T0108193

ANALECTA ROMANICA

HERAUSGEGEBEN VON FRITZ SCHALK

unter Mitwirkung von Horst Baader (Köln), Yvon Belaval (Paris),
Herbert Dieckmann (Ithaca), Hugo Friedrich (Freiburg), Wido Hempel
(Hamburg) und Erich Loos (Berlin).

Heft 34

VITTORIO KLOSTERMANN · FRANKFURT AM MAIN

DONALD STONE

FROM TALES TO TRUTHS

ESSAYS ON FRENCH FICTION IN THE
SIXTEENTH CENTURY

VITTORIO KLOSTERMANN · FRANKFURT AM MAIN

© Vittorio Klostermann Frankfurt am Main 1973
Alle Rechte, auch das der Übersetzung vorbehalten
Herstellung: Universitätsbuchdruckerei Junge & Sohn, Erlangen
Printed in Germany

PREFACE

A portion of the work presented here was done during my sabbatical leave in 1968—69, generously supported by the Guggenheim Foundation.

To Professor Naomi Miller and to the staff of Houghton Library I owe special thanks.

Cambridge, Mass.   D. S., Jr.

for
Eliot W. Nelson

CONTENTS

Introduction   9

The Unity of *Les Angoysses douloureuses*   12

Boccaccio's *Decameron* and the *Heptaméron*   21

The Aesthetics of French Humanism   29

Montreux and the Pastoral   43

Conclusion   49

Bibliography   55

INTRODUCTION

Those familiar with Gustave Reynier's *Le Roman sentimental avant l'Astrée* [1] may wish some word of explanation at the beginning of a study devoted to material already discussed by Reynier. In summary, these essays are presented to examine certain questions which Reynier himself raised or which are raised by his approach to sixteenth-century fiction.

Le Roman sentimental avant l'Astrée, taken as a whole, has distinctly negative conclusions to offer. As early as page 15, Reynier cannot resist observing about the writers he is to study: "Les auteurs semblent incapables de développer soit par l'étude directe de la vie, soit par l'interprétation des oeuvres antiques, pourtant lues et admirées, cet élément sentimental que justement alors laisse se perdre le roman d'aventures". Throughout the century, he finds either momentary glimpses of the sentimental novel to come ("Si certaines parties de l'*Heptaméron* rappellent encore la verve railleuse, irrespectueuse et même la crudité des fabliaux, on commence à s'y faire de l'amour une idée plus grave et plus haute", p. 184) or clear signs that the period had other concerns ("Comme Boccacce, la dame de Crenne abuse de la rhétorique et surtout de l'érudition", p. 114; "La *Diana* de Montemayor, traduite en 1578 par Nicole Collin, n'obtenait qu'un assez médiocre succès et ne semblait pas avoir alors d'influence", p. 167). Why these authors were incapable, why Hélisenne placed excessive emphasis on rhetoric and erudition, why France was not prepared to accept the pastoral in 1578 are also questions that Reynier did not choose to pursue. My own research has led me to believe that they are, nonetheless, central problems in the evolution of French fiction and deserving of careful examination.

If Reynier did not explore these topics it may be argued that his subject — the search for early traces of the sentimental novel in France — hardly required him to do so. But this justification only brings into focus a more fundamental problem raised by Reynier's book. If French fiction before *l'Astrée* offers little evidence of a trend

---

[1] All works referred to or quoted in the texts are cited fully in the Bibliography.

toward the sentimental novel, why was it more important to pursue a negative quest than to concentrate on an explanation of the phenomena encountered?

I would not presume to answer for Reynier; it is of some interest to note, however, that the question does not pertain to criticism on the novel alone. Until very recently studies on tragedy, too, were conceived in terms of a continuous development from *Cléopâtre captive* to Racine that brought greater glory to Classicism and a negative assessment of sixteenth-century drama. One is given the impression that had Classicism also produced a successful epic, the pattern would have been repeated a third time. Even without such a triple victory for the seventeenth century, it has always been easier to find the sixteenth century treated as the decisive, if somewhat inept, antecedent to Classicism than as the heir to fifteenth-century values or a period distinct from the worlds at either side of it.

The dominance of this pattern is all the more surprising since so much material produced by the sixteenth century prepares us to expect differences, not resemblances, between that period and French Classicism. While *plaire* was the sovereign criterion of Classicism, an overriding concern of Ronsard's century was style, an ornate and sentensious style. Listen to Du Bellay in the *Deffence*. The force of eloquence, he says, "gist aux motz propres, usitez, & non aliénes du commun usaige de parler, aux metaphores, alegories, comparaisons, similitudes, energies, & tant d'autres figures & ornemens, sans les quelz tout oraison & poëme sont nudz, manques & debiles" (pp. 35—36). Translation for Du Bellay does not capture the genius of poets, a genius which is defined by "grandeur de style, magnificence de motz, gravité de sentences, audace & varieté de figures, & mil' autres lumieres de poësie" (p. 40). Poems composed by friends of sixteenth-century dramatists lengthen the number of concerns by repeatedly singling out with the authors' eloquence their moral lessons. They had nothing to say about Aristotle, comportment, or the reworking of history — familiar preoccupations of French Classical drama.

Contemporary commentary on fiction also accentuated style and moral precepts as a measure of greatness. It was in the sixteenth century that the two major Greek novels, Heliodorus' *Aethiopian Story* and Achilles Tatius' *Loves of Clitophon and Leucippe* were first translated into French. The translators — Amyot for Heliodorus (1547), Belleforest for Achilles Tatius (1568) — use virtually the same language when extolling the qualities of the Greek texts. Agreeing with Strabo that the aim of fiction is "la delectation qui procede

10

de la nouuelleté des choses estranges", Amyot goes on to add that "entre les ieux, & passetemps de l'esprit, les plus loüables sont ceux qui oultre la resiouyssance qu'ilz nous apportent, seruent encore à limer (par maniere de dire) & affiner de plus en plus le iugement, de sorte que le plaisir n'est point du tout ocieux. Ce que i'espere que lon pourra aucunement trouuer en ceste fabuleuse histoire des amours de Chariclea, & Theagenes, en laquelle, oultre l'ingenieuse fiction, il y a quelques lieux de beaux discours tirez de la Philosophie Naturelle, & Morale: force dictz notables, & propos sentēcieux: plusieurs belles harēgues ou l'artifice d'eloquēce est tresbien employé" (π2ᵛ). On Belleforest's title page the work of Achilles Tatius is termed "Oeuure tres-vtile & delectable, où sont deduits & esclarcis plusieurs poincts, tant des histoires anciennes que de toutes les parties de la Philosophie".

These few quotations alone suggest why Hélisenne "abuse de la rhétorique" but to sense that the period enjoyed precisely what Reynier criticized[2] also underscores the need to scrutinize Reynier's general approach. If these views were widely held, if they prove to have influenced directly the creation of sixteenth-century fiction, then we can feel certain that a search for antecedents to *l'Astrée* may have bypassed much of what is characteristic of French sixteenth-century fiction. The essays to follow will, I hope, restore some measure of objectivity to a study of the material in question and bring about a fuller appreciation of its uniqueness.

---

[2] Compare also Reynier's reaction to Hélisenne's style with this judgement of a François de Bellon (1555): "Après cete noble ville de Lyon, la Picardye ne reçoit peu d'honneur de sa fille Helisenne. Les compositions de laquelle sont si souuent es mains des François se delectans de prose, qu'il n'est besoin en faire autre discours" (quoted in Demats, p. xxxiv.)

THE UNITY OF LES ANGOYSSES DOULOUREUSES

Hélisenne de Crenne — apparently the pen name of a Marguerite Briet — published her novel *Les Angoysses douloureuses qui procedent d'amours* in 1538. She divided the work into three parts and although each part is introduced by the same title given to the novel as a whole, Hélisenne made these divisions distinctive in a variety of ways. The first part is narrated by the author and treats primarily of her emotional reaction to meeting and falling in love with Guenelic. It is strongly influenced by Boccaccio's *Amorous Fiammetta*. Part Two is narrated by Guenelic, who sets out in search of Hélisenne, now locked in a tower by her indignant husband. Guenelic's adventures are shared by a friend Quezinstra and include several battles and tourneys in which Quezinstra distinguishes himself. In Part Three, still narrated by Guenelic, Hélisenne is found. Guenelic rescues her but as they make good their escape from the husband's men, Hélisenne repents, asks Guenelic to transform his physical love into a spiritual one, and dies. Quezinstra preaches to Guenelic at great length on such subjects as accepting God's will and death as liberation from earthly cares. Guenelic prays for forgiveness before he, too, dies. The work closes with an "Ample et accommodée narration" spoken by Quezinstra, who tells of the discovery of Hélisenne's book and of Mercury's arrival to take the bodies to the underworld. Quezinstra accompanies Mercury and sees Minos declare that Hélisenne and Guenelic be transported to the Elysian Fields.

Responding to these shifts in presentation and subject matter, Reynier categorized Part One as "sentimental", Part Two as "chivalric", and Part Three as "didactic", and cast doubts on Hélisenne's concern for the unity of the peculiar work she had produced: "Tel est dans son ensemble ce singulier ouvrage, si peu cohérent dans sa composition, où s'expriment tour à tour, sans craindre de s'opposer, toutes les tendances de cette époque" (p. 122).

An apparent justification for Reynier's statement is to be found in the short prefaces Hélisenne composed for Part Two and Part Three. Of Guenelic's narration to follow Hélisenne draws attention to "aulcunes oeuures belliqueuses & louables entreprinses" which, she says, we will admit "auoyr este auec vertu & magnanimite de cueur accõplyes" (AA1ᵛ). Hélisenne accentuates the apparent desire to

12

impress the reader with these events by reminding him that Alexander the Great was stirred to chivalric deeds by reading the *Iliad*. In introducing the third part Hélisenne is even more direct about her previous intention and a reorientation of her story: "... si precedentement vous ay exhorte a la discipline de lart militaire pour acquerir triumphe de renõmee, a ceste heure plus fort suis prouocquee a vous instiguer a la resistence contre vostre sensualite" (AAA2ʳ).

However, even if one read only these prefatory pieces, it would soon become clear that Hélisenne's undertaking is more complex and more coherent than Reynier suggests. For example, each preface also fixes on the continuing question of love's effect. Part Two is to pass from the "violent passions" related in Part One to "les calamitez & extremes miseres, que par indiscretement aymer les ieunes hommes peuent souffrir" (AA1ᵛ), a description, it might be noted, that can apply only to Guenelic. In the preface to Part Three, when Hélisenne signals abandonment of an exhortation to take up military discipline, she also presses us to resist sensuality, for in Part Three we will learn "de la cause par laquelle la ioye par [Guenelic] cõceue fut cõuertie en tresgriefue & cruelle passion" (AAA2ʳ).

As a result, the peculiarities in the structure of *Les Angoysses* derive not from the successive juxtaposition of completely reoriented portions of the novel but from the unexpected introduction of a call to arms into the ongoing examination of love's nefarious misfortunes and then from the equally unexpected termination of concern with "triumphe de renõmee".

It is a commonplace of criticism on *Les Angoysses* to decry the poor figure cut by Guenelic in Part Two. Hélisenne creates a chivalric context and then gives the prowess and accolades to her beloved's companion [1]. This problem, like the "incoherent" structure of the novel, arises out of our unwillingness to appreciate fully the information about her work that Hélisenne provides in the prefatory statements. From the preface to Part Two we discern a double plot: chivalric acts to inspire us and Guenelic's suffering as an indiscreet lover. "Lart militaire" is an alternative to loving and throughout Part Two Quezinstra will attempt to turn Guenelic from his love-sick mooning to the glories of war. But Guenelic refuses. Both he and Hélisenne see as an alternative to loving "indiscretement" and to suffering the calmer state of true love. Hélisenne refers to this state in her preface: "le vray naturel de ceulx qui bien ayment, est de seruir, louer & obeir" (AA2ᵛ). As Part Two opens, Guenelic has

---

[1] See Reynier, p. 119 and Demats, pp. xxv—xxxii.

already become a wiser man, recognizing that he betrayed the principles of true love. He lists the traits that a true lover must have as "magnanime, modeste, secret, soliciteux & perseuerant" (AA4^r). Between "seruir" and "perseuerant" it is not surprising why Guenelic turns a deaf ear to Quezinstra, nor why he appears in Part Two as an uninspired fighter. Time and again, the text reminds us that Guenelic is lost in thought of Hélisenne. His lack of commitment to war is proof of his devotion to love — a newly defined devotion of which Hélisenne by her own words seems to approve. Thus, the surprising element remains Hélisenne's desire to juxtapose Guenelic and Quezinstra within a context that appears just as concerned with the portrait of suffering and with Guenelic's evolution toward true love.

A simple answer would be to say that Hélisenne created Quezinstra to test Guenelic. This is too simple because it does not take into account not only the very positive statement of the author before Part Three that she did exhort the reader to "lart militaire", but also the care with which the counterarguments to love are prepared. On no fewer than five occasions in Part Two Guenelic is called upon to renounce his love.

In the first instance, Quezinstra reacts to a long lament by Guenelic in which through fourteen apostrophes the unhappy lover seeks to understand his fate and calls upon the powers to end his suffering with death. Quezinstra's argument consists of an attack against love:

> cest appetit sensuel, est vne infirmite incurable, de laquelle nayssent obliuion de Dieu & de soymesmes, perdition de temps, diminution dhonneur, discordables contentions, emulations, enuies, detractions, exilz, homicides, destruction de corps, & damnation de lame ... Toutesfoys ne vous en pouez desister, a loccasion que long temps auez plus suiuy vostre inutile volente, que la raison. (AA8^r)

He inveighs against those who see love as a god and enumerates the names of those whom such a violent love has undone. Two signatures later, the quarrel is renewed with reversed proportions. Quezinstra merely sketches his position and Guenelic is allowed to expound on the fidelity of true lovers and on all those men and women in history who exemplify the power of love. These arguments are repeated near the close of the second part in a discussion between Guenelic and a prince eager to have the knights remain with him.

On another occasion, after one of his victories on the battlefield, Quezinstra brings his arguments in line with the tenor of Hélisenne's introduction:

Gvenelic bien sommes tenuz de rendre grace auec louenge sempiter-
nelle au souuerain recteur du ciel, la vertu duquel tout luiuersel in-
forme, & en son sainct temple les armes victorieuses debuons offrir:
puis que de si noble assemblee le triũphe rapportons, plus ne debuons
craindre fortune: laquelle tant plus nous a este aduerse tant plus nous
clarifira, si nous perseuerons en vertu, car de tousiours prosperer ne
fut iamais esperit humain recommande: car en prosperite ne se pourroit sy bien demonstrer la vertu de lhõme. Alexandre Macedoniẽ sans
cõparaison eust estre collaude, si quelque foys, eust eu quelque fortune contraire: laquelle fortune ne nous a este aduerse, comme plai-
nement puis cõiecturer pour nous consumer, mais pour nous perpe-
tuer en lhabit de la vraye vertue, affin de nous exalter en triũphante
renommee & nous ascripre a limmortalite, Atropos ne scauroit em-
pescher q̃ perpetuellemẽt ne dure le noble Scipion, le cheualeureux
Camille, le victorieux Cesar, le triũphateur Auguste: desquelz les
noms sont encores florissans, qui doibt causer grand efficace & esmo-
tions aux nobles cueurs, croyant que le vray dispensateur du ciel, na
pas voulu aorner les premiers anges de gens si belliqueux. q[u'i]l ne
vueille la posterieure de semblable vertu honnorer. Lon dict le prin-
cipe de toutes choses estre la plus grãd partie. Puis doncques que
nostre commẽcement a lart militaire nous est tant felice: il ne reste
plus que de persister sans nons [sic] reduyre en ociosite: car a hõme
ocieux nulle premiation de vertu ne luy fut iamais denice. (EE7r-v)

These words were spoken, Guenelic tells us, in a fashion that outdid
"la virgilienne prononciation" (EE7v). Although they do not attack
Guenelic directly, he understands their intent. He admits to admiring
Quezinstra's will but rejects the attempt to make him "ensuiure le
martial exercice" (EE7v). In the fifth debate, Quezinstra returns to
the earlier problem of passion's sway: "Guenelic ie vous supplie q̃
mettez peine de mitiguer & temperer lacerbe douleur q[ui] si con-
tinuellement vous crucie. Et considerez q̃ si de tous accidẽtz (q[ui]
en cestuy hemisphere suruiẽnẽt) nous voulions ainsi troubler, sans q̃
la vertu de patience eust puissance de superer les passions (dont nous
sommes agitez & persecutez) iournellemẽt suruiẽdroit matiere & cause
de desepoir [sic]. Car chose ny a en ce fascheux mõde, sur laquelle
fidellemẽt fonder on se puisse . . ." (GG3r).

Quantity is not our only gauge of the importance of these remarks.
They are built upon attitudes which fill the didactic literature of
Hélisenne's day. Consider, for example, Quezinstra's portrait of love
and this definition given in Bouchet's *Les Angoysses & remedes
d'amours* (1536):

Par folle amour / on perd bon iugement /
Sens / [et] raison / . . .
. . . .
On nayme Dieu / ne (cõme on doit) son presme.
. . . .
Folle amour / est horrible maladie /
Qui tue lame / [et] consume le corps /
. . . .
En folle amour / ne verrez que discords /
Diuisions / fureur / [et] ialouzie. (pp. lv-lvi, misnumbered lxvi)

In Bouchet, too, numerous examples are given of those who have known unhappiness through love (pp. lxxi—iii) and idleness appears as the same distinct danger to virtuous living (p. xcviii).

Even more substantial a body of material to be compared to Hélisenne is provided by the emblem books which were published in France just before *Les Angoysses* or virtually at the same time. A French translation of Alciati appeared in Paris in 1536. La Perrière's *Le Theatre des bons engins,* in 1539 (printed by Denis Ianot who also sold the first edition of *Les Angoysses*), and Gilles Corrozet's *Hecatomgraphie,* in 1541 (also chez Denis Ianot).

Each of Quezinstra's major points has an equivalent formulation in one of these volumes. Three of Alciati's emblems accentuate love's great power, especially over reason (B4ᵛ, K7ᵛ, L2ᵛ). His "De Morte & Amore" (I6ᵛ) links love and misfortune. Virtue's victory over fortune resembles Corrozet's "Vertu domaine sur les astres" (B7ᵛ). The concept that adversity is meant to test such "vertu", "si nous perseuerons", had already been expressed by Alciati's "Virtuti fortuna comes" (C7ᵛ) and "Ex arduis perpetuum nomen" (D4ᵛ) and would be repeated by La Perrière after his ninety-seventh emblem: "Vertu se preuue en mal plus qu'aultrement, / Elle florist en temps d'aduersité". Alciati, too, denounced idleness (C3ᵛ). The concepts that patience must dominate passion, that there is nothing in this world in which man can place his trust constitute two of the most familiar commonplaces of emblem literature: Alciati, "Semper praesto esse infortunia" (G4ᵛ), La Perrière, LV "L'homme prudent en moderation, / Ce qu'il pretend, fait successiuement", Corrozet, "Chasteté vaincq Cupido" (C5ᵛ), "Toutes choses sont perissables" (G4ᵛ), "Le monde instable" (G5ᵛ).

The amount of resemblance here is too great to be fortuitous. It shows that *Les Angoysses* belongs to a tradition of didactic literature, that Hélisenne's various pronouncements about a moral purpose were taken as seriously by her in prefacing the book as they must be by us in examining it. Viewed against the background of that didactic literature, the sudden emergence of a call to renown loses its peculiarity. The principles of true love which Guenelic originally betrays represent only an accomodation, an attitude that will not suffice before those who mistrust the emotions. For them the misfortunes of love demonstrate that love itself must be considered a misfortune and in creating Quezinstra Hélisenne provided her novel with the full range of contemporary attitudes toward love. At the same time, since we are concerned with structure here, it should be noted that in a more limited way Hélisenne had already accomplished this in Part One by drawing a double portrait of herself as Hélisenne the lover and Hélisenne the sinner.

The debates between Guenelic and Quezinstra are more fully developed but from her earliest pages Hélisenne formulates a discussion of love that contrasts love and moral behavior. Here is a sampling of her objective attitude toward her actions: chapter III, "Alors ie commencay a vser de regardz impudicques, delaissant toute crainte & vergoigne"; IV, "iestoye deuenue hardye, & audacieuse"; XI, "La cause de mon pleur ne me procedoit de la iuste douleur & remordz de conscience qne [sic] ie debuoye anoyr [sic] de ma vie detestable, car au moyen que iauoye chasse raison, tousiours depuis cestoit monstree de moy loingtaine & fugetiue."

Despite such objectivity, she persists, as does Guenelic in Part Two. Their perseverance may have some function within the framework of true love, but as regards the total evolution of the book, it succeeds admirably in reinforcing the belief of Quezinstra, the emblem books, and Hélisenne herself that love is a powerful force which blinds reason. In this justification for Quezinstra's exhortations, we also find the reason for their failure and disappearance. They summarize a rational position on love which must inevitably fall outside the world of the lovers. Quezinstra reasons according to another logic, feels obliged to obey other principles.

The inability of the lovers to fight against the force of love reveals that a solution must be sought elsewhere, that is, in the reorientation of Part Three. For two thirds of the work, reason and passion war, unsuccessfully, perhaps because they appear such equal, if antithetical forces. Part Three provides a solution because it removes the argument to a plane which is above human logic and passion.

The opening of Part Three constitutes a momentary return of love's logic unchallenged. Although a religious man begs Guenelic to abandon "ceste lasciuité" (AAA4ᵛ) and warns him that his love will know an unhappy end, Hélisenne devotes as much space to an eloquent *apologia* of the perfect lover spoken by Guenelic. In a step by step analysis, Guenelic shows how the perfect lover refrains from each of the seven deadly sins. Later, upon his discovery of Hélisenne, he admits to his imperfect behavior and summarizes his past difficulties which he suffered in her service. We seem to be advancing toward the triumph, not the condemnation of passion until men sent by Hélisenne's husband pursue the pair and their faithful companion. Hélisenne is separated from the warring groups and when Guenelic finds her, she exclaims, "par ce qui ie nesperoye de iamais te veoir, iay este par angoisseuse douleur tant affligee & trauaillee, quil nest en ma faculte de pouuoir exhiber. Et auec ce, ay este tãt agitee de liurnalle froidure, q̃ icelle peine corporelle cõgregee auec les passyõs de lame mont tãt p[er]secutee q̃ ie sens de moy approcher les troys seurs lesquelles immaturemẽt le fil vital me copperont" (DDD2ᵛ).

Death, it would seem, plays the *Deus ex machina*. In truth, Hélisenne has a much more sophisticated plan, one in which death permits the author to invoke what Bouchet had already declared to be the ultimate cure for passion: repentance and purification[2]. Hélisenne makes a public confession ("ie accuse ma vituperation & torpitude, & deteste mes vices", DDD3ᵛ) and bids Guenelic to love her soul as he once loved her body if they are to experience the promise of salvation. Guenelic will agree, as his final words — also a confession of past sins — testify, but not before he is made to accept through Quezintra's argumentation the inevitability of death as "le vouloir du sublime & puissant Dieu" (DDD6ᵛ).

Thus, to Reynier's incoherent composition we can oppose a finely drawn dialectic in which the successive stages follow carefully each other and never betray the general intent announced. Each stage — Hélisenne's double portrait of herself, Guenelic's debates with Quezintra, the final death scene — bears directly on a description of the misfortunes of love just as the arrival in Elysium signals the victory of virtue over vice. All the attitudes on love expressed, for and against, on true love as well as passion, belong to that same description since the attacks on love continually feed on the stance adopted by the lovers. It may seem paradoxical to some, but when in the title of her "epistre dedicative" Hélisenne tells her readers that she is

---

[2] Under the general heading "Des Remedes contre folle amour", he writes, "Il fault premier qua Dieu on shumilie / ... Secondement fouyr (ce qui plus lye) / A folle amour" (p. xcii).

exhorting them "a bien & hõnestement aymer, en euitant toute vaine & impudique amour" (A2ᵛ), she is following through that promise at the very moment that she and her lover turn a deaf ear to the voices that seek to dissuade them.

One clue to Reynier's reasoning on the structure of *Les Angoysses* can be found in his suggestion that when passing from the sentimental to the chivalric and finally to the religious, Hélisenne tried her hand at "toutes les tendances de cette époque". He appears to have meant literary trends and to have seen each trend as a separate genre. A close analysis of *Les Angoysses* would reveal rather that these "trends" were in Hélisenne's eyes only a means to the general end of moralizing about love. The "chivalric" portion shares little with the world of medieval romances or with the contemporary *Amadis de Gaule*. Love and adventure do not alternate as in *Amadis*; the tourneys and battles are only a backdrop against which Hélisenne is eager to develop a confrontation of views on love and life. Similarly, if the subject matter of Part Three is religious in orientation, it follows not as a disjunctive addition but as an aspect of the traditional debate on love which has always been present[3] yet only now becomes operative. (Hélisenne's concern about salvation offers a particularly good example of the transformation.) The structural unity of *Les Angoysses* is but a reflection of Hélisenne's unity of purpose and her adherence to a tradition that emphasized moralizing, not genres.

Reynier was right to be struck by Hélisenne's neologisms and her erudition, but he was content to present them as facts, not clues. Through this emphasis on style we can see that there is an affinity in *Les Angoysses* not only between Hélisenne and the somewhat simple didactic literature of the day such as emblem books but also between Hélisenne and the world of French and Italian humanism. Here, the union of moral purpose and elegant expression so carefully described by Quintilian had acquired fresh meaning as more and more classical texts became available. Erasmus provides an excellent formulation of the way in which style and instruction were joined in the mind of the humanist when he states at the beginning of his *De ratione studii*: "All knowledge falls into one of two divisions: the knowledge of 'truths' and the knowledge of 'words': and if the former is first in importance the latter is acquired first in order of time. They are not

---

[3] I think of Hélisenne's phrase from chapter XI of Part One, quoted above, p. 17, which uses the phrase "remordz de conscience" and of the important religious phrases in a speech from Part Two, quoted in the essay on The Aesthetics of French Humanism, p. 35.

to be commended who, in their anxiety to increase their store of truths, neglect the necessary art of expressing them" (quoted in Woodward, p. 162). Hélisenne's neologisms and her erudition constitute a portion, but only a portion, of "the necessary art" of expressing the truths contained in *Les Angoysses*.

Hélisenne's editor Paule Demats has observed that in two particular instances the style of Part One reveals "de véritables centons": Guenelic's letter and Hélisenne's laments (p. xxiv). It is not surprising that the author should have borrowed so heavily here since these passages, much more than the narrative, were recognized rhetorical pieces requiring the most effective turn of phrase in order to move (and instruct) the reader.

The same sensitivity to an elegant style may appear in passages that bear no relationship to a moral purpose. In the *Fiammetta*, Boccaccio exhibited the humanists' enjoyment of mythological circumlocutions to indicate the time or season as in "Le Soleil estoit desia tourné vne fois, en la part du ciel, qui se brusla lors que le presomptueux fils guida mal son char, depuis que Pampile estoit departy de moy" (f. 287^r). Hélisenne does likewise repeatedly, sometimes mixing the elegant neologisms with straightforward narration: "Mais quãd laurigateur du celeste char ses cheuaulx baynez en locean commencoit a haulcer, ie fuz mandee pour aller parler à mõ mary . . ." (G8^v). In the middle of a dramatic request that her husband transfix her with his sword, Hélisenne cries, "Ne vser de pitie en moy nõ plus que feist Pirrhus en Polisenne, laquelle fut immolee sur le tũbeau de Achilles" (B5^r). In both cases the contrast between style and moment is striking. To any reader concerned about verisimilitude, Hélisenne's neologisms or erudition seem suited neither to the pedestrian content of the first passage nor to the tensions of the second. But again her "excesses" prove a valuable clue, showing us to what degree style and moralizing, not verisimilitude, were uppermost in the mind of the author. They even determine much of the presentation of the characters. Hélisenne's objectivity, like Quezinstra's prowess or Guenelic's constancy, are not what we would call today character traits. They are fundamentals of the argumentation which have been given a human shape.

Ultimately, then, Hélisenne's purpose is indistinguishable from her aesthetics. We are not discussing a work in which occasional literary devices are enlisted to underscore its message. Because moralizing and rhetoric were inextricably joined in contemporary understanding of Quintilian's *Institutio oratoria*, the message brings with it a technique and rhetoric pervades the book at all levels. The observation

that Quezinstra spoke with "la virgilienne prononciation" is but a
significant point of departure that leads us back to structure and to
unity. Since rhetoric includes the art of disputation as well as the
careful use of words, the structure we have uncovered in Hélisenne's
divided portrait of herself or in the opposition between Guenelic and
Quezinstra within the dialectic that relates all three sections of the
novel leaves no doubt that rhetoric's principles guided Hélisenne
when she constructed her novel. It will be interesting to see if it is
also possible to identify Hélisenne's technique elsewhere in the prose
of the period.

BOCCACCIO'S DECAMERON AND THE HEPTAMERON

It is Marguerite de Navarre herself who suggests that she may have
been influenced by Boccaccio. She commissioned Antoine Le Maçon
to translate the *Decameron* into French; in the prologue of her own
Heptaméron she lists "madame Marguerite" among those members
of the French court who enjoyed reading the *Decameron* and who
once contemplated imitating the work of the Italian *brigata*. Critical
literature on her short stories has often taken the next step and spoken
of a definite influence. Pierre Jourda states that "L'influence des conteurs italiens éclate à chaque page de l'*Heptaméron*: la disposition du
livre, le décor, le souci d'art, le désir très net de substituer à la peinture des scènes simplement plaisantes l'analyse des sentiments et des
passions, la forme même de la nouvelle, autant d'emprunts de Marguerite à la technique des conteurs italiens" (II, 680).

At the same time, exhaustive searching by Jourda brought this
student of the Queen of Navarre to the conclusion that Marguerite
borrowed nothing specific from Boccaccio save the framework for her
tales (II, 688). To date no one has come forth to challenge this conclusion or to help us deal adequately with the mystery of Marguerite's
rather slim debt to a work she nevertheless read and admired. The
following essay is intended to show what light may be shed on that
mystery through a comparison of the elements of intention and
execution in the two works.

Regarding Boccaccio and the purpose of his hundred tales, the most
intriguing aspect of the work is its refusal to call constant attention
to its educational value. Although a few phrases can be found in the

21

Decameron which point to a longstanding association in the world of letters between the *novella* and moral instruction [1], they are not numerous. Moreover, the remarks of the author contained in a preface, a prologue to the fourth day, and a conclusion take us even farther from such a perspective. The preface promises that "sweetness and delight" will follow the terrible portrait of the plague. The prologue takes up certain criticisms addressed to Boccaccio and suggests that many readers of the first three days, too, expected the *novella* to instruct and to exhibit lofty ambitions in its style as well as content. Some, notes Boccaccio, have dismissed his "preoccupation with women and their entertainment" as "nonsense"; others have said that "[he'd] be wiser to spend [his] time with the Muses on Parnassus, than to fritter it away among [the ladies], with such trifles" (pp. 220—21).

Boccaccio's reply is at best ambiguous. He tells a story which he uses to illustrate the loveliness of women and to justify his preoccupation with them. The moral lesson that "it takes superhuman strength to violate [the laws of nature]" (p. 225) is strangely detached from the tale although it is one which will underlie several stories in the *Decameron*. Boccaccio mentions the moral some paragraphs later, does not insist upon it, but hurries to return to the storytelling. The same ambiguity appears when Boccaccio speaks of the muses ("Perhaps even in the writing of these stories, humble though they be, they may have come, sometimes, to keep me company", p. 224) and when he presents his conclusion. There Boccaccio reminds us that his tales were not told "by clerics or philosophers in any church or school, but in gardens and places of recreation" (p. 663). On the other hand, the conclusion assures us that if "any wishes to derive use or benefit from them, they will not prevent him" (p. 664).

Interestingly enough, this attitude is reflected in the behavior of the girls who belong to the *brigata*. In the main Boccaccio's ladies remain discreetly aloof and thus detached from the stories. On occasion, we are told that reactions differed (pp. 604, 659) — a possible stimulus to Marguerite to add as she did a discussion by the group after each tale — but Boccaccio refrains from giving us any hint of what was said. When a story's content is slightly offcolor or controversial, the ladies' reaction is rendered by remarks like: "they chided him prettily, pretending such naughty stories were not the sort to tell

---

[1] "Good examples are always useful, dear ladies, and should be listened to with a wide-awake mind, no matter who tells them" (p. 33). "We should never tire of listening to examples, whether we're happy or miserable, for the happy are made wary, and the miserable, comforted" (p. 77).

in the presence of women" (p. 22); "Filiostrato had not been able to veil his remarks about the Parthian fillies so skillfully, but that the knowing ladies had laughed, pretending to be amused by something else" (p. 399). After the second story of the ninth day we are told that "all the ladies had rendered thanks to God for so felicitous a rescue of the young nun from the fangs of her envious sisters" (p. 324) — a statement that only appears to commit the girls. For, although the young nun has been censured by a superior no less guilty than she, the reaction just quoted carefully avoids the more fundamental fact that both nuns have violated the vow of chastity.

Perplexing, such prudery and detachment also run counter to the tone of Boccaccio's own conclusion: "Even if there should be some little passage or word a little too strong to be stomached by your virtuous, sainted spinsters who place more stock in words than in deeds, and strive more to create the impression of goodness than to practice it themselves, I should no more be condemned for using them than one would condemn people in general for bandying all day long such words as *hole* and *peg, mortar* and *pestle, sausage* and *bologna,* and all kinds of things of the same import" (p. 663). I have no ready explanation for such complexities; their value to us here lies in the total contrast in technique between the *Decameron* and the *Heptaméron.*

That Marguerite used the *Heptaméron* to express certain concepts on love and religion which were of importance to her is a fact too well established to require any further comment. At the same time, the elaboration of her moral scheme brought her a considerable distance from the world of the *Decameron.* The relationship between the tales and the storytellers, for example, is radically changed.

Marguerite's tales are not always pristine. Yet, when the content is in questionable taste, the characters, male and female, may confront the issue directly and sometimes insure that it is resolved in a manner consonant with the overall intent to analyze human conduct. Oisille labels the eleventh tale "ord et salle", but adds, "congnoissant les personnes à qui il est advenu, on ne le sçauroit trouver fascheux" (p. 89). More important is the discussion following tale 52. The narrator recognizes that it was not "clean" but Hircan observes that "les parolles ne sont jamais puantes". Oisille agrees. However, if the words they just heard are not offensive, "il y en a d'autres que l'on appelle *villaines,* qui sont de mauvaise odeur, quant l'ame est plus faschée que le corps..." (p. 334). The tale itself is quite forgotten and the *devisants* discuss whether the female reaction to such "villaines" words bespeaks virtue or hypocrisy.

A more obvious innovation by Marguerite is the principle that all the tales should be true stories. There are several reasons for believing that it had roots in France's concept of the word *nouvelle,* which appears to have held the modern connotations of "new" and "news".

The preface to the *Cent Nouvelles Nouvelles* condemns the use of the word in the *Decameron* since many of Boccaccio's tales treat of ancient times. It promises the reader only fresh and contemporary material. When Bonaventure des Periers presented his *Nouvelles Récréations* in 1558, he echoed these sentiments and added an explanation that parallels closely Marguerite's explanation of that preference for true tales which was held by the French court and taken up by her own *devisants:* "Les nouvelles qui viennent de si loingtain pays, avant qu'elles soyent rendues sus le lieu, ou elles souspirent comme le saffran, ou s'encherissent comme les draps de soye, ou il s'en pert la moytié comme d'espiceries, ou se buffetent comme les vins, ou sont falsifiées comme les pierreries, ou sont adulterées comme tout" [2]. As it is integrated by Marguerite with the body of her work, the principle heightens our awareness of the interaction of the *devisants* and their material and of the moral thrust that pervades the volume.

The *devisants* engage in much banter, especially between men and women. At the end of the second day, Saffredent tells a story critical of the ladies. He then selects Parlamente to tell the next tale saying, "elle fera mectre en obly la verité que je vous ay dicte" (p. 157). This appears just more banter; however, as the discussions evolve, it becomes clear that verities revealed may not be forgotten here. They are to be recognized as such and accepted. Had not Oisille already exclaimed, "Et si ce n'estoit que nous avons tous juré de dire verité, je ne sçauroys croyre que une femme de l'estat dont elle estoit, sceut estre si meschante de l'ame ..." (pp. 154—55)? Through acceptance come tolerance and candor so that even deeper truths are spoken by the *devisants.* They may refer to themselves: "Et", says Saffredent, in a particularly animated discussion, "si nous voulons dire verité, il n'y a nul de nous qui n'ait experimenté ceste furieuse follye" (p. 265), or to others. When Hircan hesitates to speak about an evil lady, Oisille tells him that since they have sworn to tell the truth, the others must listen to him, "car les maulx que nous disons des

[2] Quoted in A. J. Krailsheimer, *Three Sixteenth-Century Conteurs,* (New York and Oxford, 1966), p. 93. See also C. V. Livingston, "The *Heptaméron des Nouvelles* of Marguerite de Navarre: A Study of Nouvelles 28, 34, 52 and 62," *Romanic Review* XIV (1923), 97—100.

hommes et des femmes ne sont poinct pour la honte particulliere de ceulx dont est faict le compte, mais pour oster l'estime de la confiance des creatures, en monstrant les miseres où ilz sont subgectz, afin que nostre espoir s'arreste et s'appuye à Celluy seul qui est parfaict et sans lequel tout homme n'est que imperfection" (p. 317).

Oisille's words deserve to be read carefully. Their meaning is plain; their implications for Marguerite's technique, capital. The revelations about particular characters in the *nouvelles* are not to be our main concern. They only serve to illustrate ("en monstant") the overconfidence of all mankind ("l'estime de la confiance des creatures"), providing thereby the general lesson which must inspire us to put our faith in God. Thus, if there is greater involvement between *nouvelle* and *devisant* in the *Heptaméron* than between their counterparts in the *Decameron*, the relationship as defined by Oisille resembles more nearly Hélisenne's extraction of moral truths from various human situations than analyses of particular circumstances. The text upholds what Oisille describes and there is no better way to sense how Marguerite places truth over tale than to juxtapose story and discussion.

On certain occasions, a rather empty tale launches a very serious and prolonged discussion. Stories 34 and 44, for example, relate short anecdotes about the Cordeliers. The first *nouvelle* gives rise nevertheless to words on Plato, passion, and salvation; in the second case, to contemplation of preachers.

Elsewhere, the discrepancy between story and discussion becomes startling because of a reverse process. The story is rich in insight into human emotion whereas the discussion bypasses and even downgrades this richness. In story 12 Dagousin tells the tale of Lorenzo de Medici's murder of the Duke of Florence. The text stresses Lorenzo's dilemma: to save the honor of his sister and family, endangered by the Duke's whims, or betray his obligation to the Duke, his prince and benefactor. It stresses also the courage of the Duke when attacked by Lorenzo and Lorenzo's "mauvaise conscience" after the crime. Yet Dagousin opens the discussion by warning the ladies against Cupid who makes both high and low forget God. The phrase refers to the Duke. Lorenzo is alluded to, but only through an equally succinct aphorism: those in authority, says Dagousin, should beware of displeasing those beneath them. The group then divides in opinion. The women uphold Lorenzo for protecting his sister; the men condemn him for killing his prince. No one exhibits concern over the complexity of Lorenzo' situation. Quite the contrary, as soon as the group splits in its judgment of Lorenzo, Dagousin intervenes, "Pour Dieu, mes dames, ne prenez poinct querelle d'une chose desja passée; mais gardez que voz beaultez ne facent poinct faire de plus cruels meurdres que celluy que j'ay compté" (p. 95). The intervention succeeds in turning the *devisants* away from the tale and the remainder of the discussion involves only general parrying by the women and the men.

The thirtieth *nouvelle* is a strange tale of incest that ends in the marriage of a boy with his own child. In addition to stressing the sin of the mother who slept with her son, Hircan gives a very human portrait of her sorrow. Here are the final lines of the tale: (The boy and his wife have settled in the mother's house.) "Ilz continuerent tousjours en ceste grande amityé, et la pauvre dame, en son extresme penitence, ne les voyoit jamais faire bonne chere, qu'elle ne se retirast pour pleurer" (p. 233). In that portion of the discussion which treats of the tale, not one *devisant* exhibits compassion for the characters. Again, all who comment move immediately to the moral plane and reduce the story to an example of human frailty.

The fortieth *nouvelle* must be among the most moving of the book. It begins in a fashion reminiscent of certain *Decameron* tales destined to underscore the force of nature's laws but quickly evolves toward the kind of revelation and predicament characteristic of the moral that impresses Oisille. A miserly brother refuses to marry his sister in order to escape paying her dowry. In the same household the brother is served by a young man so excellent in character that he often says he wished he could have the servant for a brother-in-law. This thought is repeated with such frequency that the couple contracts a secret marriage, certain in their own minds that were they ever discovered, they would be forgiven. Instead, after many years of happiness, the brother is apprised of the affair and has the man murdered even though his sister reveals the marriage. The tale contains a moving speech by the sister who asks her brother for death and indications that the brother much regretted his crime. Still, out of fear, he imprisons her in a castle where she passes her final years in saintly devotion. From all this Parlamente draws the lesson that one should not marry without the consent of one's parents. Oisille agrees. Nomerfide even goes so far as to find the sister's happy years more than adequate compensation for her misfortune: "J'estime ce contentement si grand, qu'il me semble qu'il passe l'ennuy qu'elle porta" (p. 278). Only Longarine appears concerned about the tragedy, "Ne faictes-vous poinct cas de la honte qu'elle receut . . . et de sa prison" (p. 279), to which Nomerfide gives this singular (and abstract) answer: "J'estime . . . que la personne qui ayme parfaictement d'un amour joinct au commandement de son Dieu, ne congnoist honte ni deshonneur,

26

sinon quant elle default ou diminue de la perfection de son amour . . .
et, quant à la prison de son corps, je croy que, pour la liberté de son
cueur, qui estoit joinct à Dieu et à son mary, ne la sentoit poinct . . ."
(p. 279). This is, in effect, a rewriting of the tale, not an analysis of
the givens. Nomerfide seizes upon the question as an opportunity to
tell Longarine (and the reader) how it is possible to escape the tribu-
lations the sister may have known. A variation on Oisille's comment
that tales should produce lessons, this more personal philosophy succeeds just as fully in reducing the story to an element of secondary
importance.

Since these discussions constitute Marguerite's recognized innovation within a framework analogous to the *Decameron*, what we have
just seen points to the disturbing conclusion that the many portraits
of human emotion which have impressed critics of the *Heptaméron*
did not matter particularly to Marguerite, who, through the *devisants'*
observations, reduced their scope and depth. On the other hand, such
a devaluation brings the total work more in harmony with Krailsheimer's recent hypothesis that after the fifth day Marguerite's intent
was to make the tales more like "the traditional exemplum" [3]. There
are other indications as well.

Krailsheimer mentions Marguerite's haste and points to certain
mistakes in the text. Such mistakes exist before the sixth day. They
are not numerous but they are perplexing if we want to believe that
Marguerite gave considerable thought to the literary expression in
her stories [4].

Near the close of the thirteenth *nouvelle*, Marguerite wrote "la
dame . . . avoit tant d'envye de rire, veu que de sa tromperie estoit sailly
ung tel bien" (p. 107). Yet the narrator of the story warns the others
shortly thereafter that "ne fault poinct accuser ceste dame de tromperie, mais estimer de son bon sens" (p. 108). As tale 25 is closing,
Longarine calls what she is reciting orally "ce qu'elle m'a faict mettre
icy en escript" (p. 206) [5]. When the moral of story 8 is formulated
before the tale is told, Longarine announces that it will show how
easily women are deceived. As the story evolves, however, the wife
gains the upper hand on her husband and Longarine opens the dis-

---

[3] A. J. Krailsheimer, "The Heptameron Reconsidered," p. 85.

[4] Compare: "Il y a dans l'*Heptaméron* un indéniable souci de la composition:
Marguerite a voulu offrir au lecteur un livre médité, préparé, composé," Jourda,
Marguerite d'Angoulême, II, 682.

[5] The variant, "telle que je l'ay mise icy par escrit," does nothing to correct
the problem.

cussion with this salvo against the men: "Il me semble, mes dames, que, si tous ceulx qui ont faict de pareilles offences à leurs femmes estoient pugniz de pareille pugnition, Hircan and Saffredent devroient avoir belle paour" (p. 47).

By the same token, if careless about moments in the text and seemingly often unimpressed by her own tales as human portraits, Marguerite did not hesitate to inject into her characters moral sentiments commensurate with the sententious quality of many discussions. I speak not so much of Dame Oisille, Parlamente, and Dagousin, whose neoplatonic or *évangélique* ideas are well known, but of Geburon, Saffredent, and especially of that Gallic spirit Hircan. In the prologue, after Oisille replies to the question of what pastime to recommend by discussing the value of scriptural reading, of all the *devisants* it is Hircan who observes: "Ma dame, ceulx qui ont leu la saincte Escripture, comme je croy que nous tous avons faict, confesseront, que vostre dict est tout veritable" (p. 8). He proposes another pastime, not in lieu of reading the Bible, which they will do in the morning, but to supplement it and the evidence of the text that follows amply demonstrates that the group *has* acquired familiarity with the Bible. After story 22 Geburon quotes St. Paul. After story 36 Saffredent quotes St. John. After story 48 Ennasuite quotes St. James. Within the narration of the thirtieth *nouvelle* Hircan is made to observe: "Mais, en lieu de se humillier et recongnoistre l'impossibilité de nostre chair, qui sans l'ayde de Dieu ne peult faire que peché, voulant par elle-mesmes et par ses larmes satisfaire au passé et par sa prudence eviter le mal de l'advenir, donnant tousjours l'excuse de son peché à l'occassion et non à la malice, à laquelle n'y a remede que la grace de Dieu, pensa de faire chose parquoy à l'advenir ne sçauroit plus tumber en tel inconvenient" (p. 231), a tone he maintains by commencing the discussion with a quotation from the Psalms.

How far we have come from the *Decameron,* and although it has always been easy to ascribe such remarks to Marguerite's own religious views, the evidence of *Les Angoysses* demonstrates that Marguerite was not alone at the time in mixing fiction with the moral preoccupations of French humanism. There are further parallels between the *Heptaméron* and *Les Angoysses* with respect to their treatment of source material. Marguerite effaces Boccaccio's ambiguities in the presentation of his material; so, too, Hélisenne follows *Amorous Fiammetta* only in Part One and pursues her dialectic to a resolution. Boccaccio's story ends with Fiammetta's wish that her book may serve as an example to the happy of the misfortunes they must avoid.

28

But she has also just maintained that she should not be censured since her only fault was "to be young and tender". Moreover, she sees her suffering as never experienced before: hardly a practical or a moral resolution of her tale.

Singular differences as well as resemblances exist between *Les Angoysses* and the *Heptaméron*. The many-sided influence of rhetoric on Hélisenne cannot be applied equally to the *Heptaméron*, but for that very reason the *Heptaméron* adds an interesting dimension to our study. The *Heptaméron* shows that with or without the specifics of humanist style fiction in France was for many wedded to didacticism, to a perspective on its material that had to come between Marguerite and Boccaccio regardless of the nature or depth of her appreciation for what had been accomplished in the *Decameron*. I do not find it surprising that the Italian tales are not reset by Marguerite. When she can repeatedly reduce complex human situations to pithy truths, she reminds us that the moral always meant more to the period than its vehicle. Her admiration for Boccaccio's storytelling was doubtlessly genuine. Yet it may have signified primarily that through the *Decameron* she was made aware of the *novella's* potential for communicating the truths she felt so strongly and the educated world expected [6].

THE AESTHETICS OF FRENCH HUMANISM

As the sixteenth century advanced, it produced texts in ever increasing numbers which suggest that, in France at least, the value of a work of fiction was directly related to its style, its erudition, its "utility", that is, its moralizing.

Marguerite's technique in the *Heptaméron* becomes doubly revealing when compared to Le Maçon's presentation of the newly translated *Decameron*: "Et quant aux autres qui vouldront dire, que ie deuoye despendre le temps à traduire quelque autre liure de plus grand fruict, i'employeray pour moy en cest endroit, ce que Bocace dict au proesme de sa quatriesme iournée, & à la conclusion de son liure ou ie les remectz. Les asseurant bien qu'ilz ne veirent par

---

[6] For a somewhat different approach to Marguerite which nonetheless also accentuates differences between Marguerite and the *Decameron*, see Janet Ferrier's stimulating study *Forerunners of the French Novel*, (Manchester, 1955), pp. 89-92.

aduenture de leur vie œuure de plaisir d'ou lon peust plus cueillir de fruict qu'on fera de ceste cy, s'ilz l'y veullent bien cercher [*sic*]" (ã2ᵛ).

Judging by his prologue to his translation of Heliodorus, Amyot was not well disposed toward works which lacked verisimilitude but when referring to medieval French books which had mixed fiction and fact, he rejects them not only for this lack of verisimilitude but also because "il n'y a nulle erudition, nulle cognoissance de l'antiquité, ne chose aucune (à brief parler) dont on peust tirer quelque vtilité" (π2ᵛ).

Although such voicings by the humanists did not prevent the period from enjoying *Amadis de Gaule,* it is interesting to hear the first French translator of *Amadis,* Nicolas d'Herberay, praise the pleasure to be gained from the book "combien que ce qui s'offre en ceste traduction d'Amadis, ne soit tiré de nul auteur fameux pour luy donner couleur de verité" (ã3ᵛ). To return to more positive statements, we find Laudun d'Aigaliers writing of Nicolas de Montreux, author of tragedies and novels: "C'est ce brave Français qui, par toute la France /A contre l'ignorance et le vice combattu" (quoted in Daele, pp. 152—53).

All critics have not believed that the period took such remarks seriously. Reynier wrote of Belleforest's claims to instruct in the *Histoires Tragiques:* "Il semble que les lecteurs aient été assez insensibles à cette intention moralisatrice et qu'ils aient surtout cherché dans les *Histoires Tragiques* ce que le titre promettait, c'est-à-dire des péripéties violentes et des dénouements brutaux" (p. 164). The case for associating literary tastes during the religious wars with an attraction to violence was given new support by studies on the baroque [1]. I am not convinced that the presence of violence in literature of this period need be equated with a new aesthetic, however.

Reynier does not cite any text to substantiate his theory but he does quote Jacques Yver in support of the idea that the *Histoires Tragiques* were extremely popular during the religious wars. The *Histoires Tragiques* have acquired, says Yver, "tant de grace qu'aujourd'huy c'est une honte entre les filles bien nourries et entre les mieux apprins courtisans de les ignorer, mesmes que ceux qui n'en peuvent orner leur langue, en ornent à tout le moins leurs mains par contenance" (Reynier, p. 162). The quotation can tell us even more. Yver singles out two distinct categories for which a knowledge of the *Histoires Tragiques* is essential. Both categories — "filles bien nour-

---

[1] See in particular Jean Rousset's *La Littérature de l'âge baroque en France,* (Paris, 1953).

ries" and "les mieux apprins courtisans" — are defined in such a way as to give no hint whatsoever of a taste for violence. Rather, the adjectives intimate a relation between the *Histoires Tragiques* and education. This supposition is supported by the phrase "orner leur langue". Admittedly, this might be an elegant circumlocution for "slip into conversation"; however, "nourries", "apprins", and "orner" together suggest that the education in question was not exclusively social but included those moral principles that Belleforest offered specifically to guide young ladies [2] and which the humanists but also the society of the time associated with elegant discourse [3].

Secondly, it is worth giving some attention to Belleforest's own comments on the content of the tales. When preparing the reader for the last story of his first volume of translations, Belleforest alludes directly to the tragedies in the *Histoires*. Nothing betrays lip service to moralizing or concealed enjoyment of violence: "Les tragiques euenemens des malheurs humains, quoy qu'au recit de leur amertume, & degoust ils apportent, ie ne sçay quel desdain fascheux & deplaisir incroyable, ci gist pourtant sous l'escorce de cest aloes vn miel plus doux que la mesme douceur, pour le fruict que la posterité en peut tirer" (I, 690).

A third dimension of these works that must be considered when speaking of violent plots is the uniformity of French humanist writing throughout the century. Such uniformity was fostered by the fact that the sixteenth century in France spent little time with the theory of genres and produced *arts poétiques* which differentiated among genres primarily in terms of form, style, and social station of the characters whereas wide reading in the period reveals that long after Hélisenne produced her novel, French humanists remained concerned about stylistic display and a didactic tone.

---

[2] Compare these remarks, part of Belleforest's introduction to the second tale of the second volume of the *Histoires Tragiques:* "Les filles de Rome iadis viuoyent recluses dans les palais de leurs peres, estans tousiours à la queüe des meres, & toutefois estoyent elles si bien instruites, que les plus ciuilisees, & mieux aprises des nostres, auroyent assez affaire à secōder vne des moins parfaites. Mais que peuuent aprendre de ciuil, & tant bon, nos filles en ce temps par les compagnies, que des paroles pleines de paillardises & lubricité, des gestes remplis de bouffonne-rie: & le plus souuent des actes qui sont moins honnestes, que la parole ne sçauroit l'exprimer" (II, 75).

[3] See in particular the very popular *Thresor des Livres d'Amadis de Gaule*, in which speeches, letters, and lamentations from the novel are reproduced for "le bon esprit" who is to find there "le moyen & grace de harenguer, concionner, par-ler, & escrire de tous affaires qui s'offriront deuant ses yeux..." (Lyons, 1571), p. 4.

The censure of idleness is continued in this gloss which accompanied certain printings of the *Histoires Tragique*: "Oisiveté nourrice de paillardise" (quoted in Hook, p. 16). In his *Tragédie de Radégonde,* Du Souhait placed this Bouchetlike definition of love:

> L'Amour cause la mort des hommes les plus braues
> L'Amour par ses effets rend les libres esclaues.
> L'Amour fait renuerser les plus riches citez,
> L'Amour est cause en fin de nos aduersitez. (p. 21)

The writers frequently repeat key moments of debate and philosophizing. The situation created by Hélisenne in the early pages of Part Two, where Quezinstra attempts to turn Guenelic from love of his lady and failing to do so, agrees to help Guenelic find her, was reproduced in more than one tragedy [4].

Even the attitude toward source material is substantially unchanged. Although it may appear to a modern reader that violence characterizes Bandello's stories to which Belleforest added long rhetorical speeches, an objective comparison of the Italian and French texts would show that much of the rhetorical material existed already in Bandello [5]. In fact, it is just as plausible to believe that Boaystuau and Belleforest were attracted to the rhetorical side of Bandello as to his violent portraits.

With respect to style and moralizing, it would not be an exaggeration to say that the second half of the century outdid the first half. However much the years of the religious wars may appear to have known constant disruption, the fact remains that it was also the period of Ronsard's *Sonnets pour Hélène,* Desportes' *Premières Oeuvres,* and Garnier's tragedies, indeed, of a veritable burgeoning of tragedy [6]. Moreover, through such works was established a literary tradition that lasted well into the seventeenth century, that is, well beyond any taste for violence which might have been sustained by the wars.

---

[4] In, for example, Le Sieur d'Aves' *Tragédie de sainte Agnès* and Garnier's *Hippolyte.*

[5] See in T. G. Griffith's *Bandello's Fiction,* (Oxford, 1955), pp. 82—83 the brief discussion of Bandello's adaptation of the Sophonisba legend. It shows, says Griffith, "Bandello's tendency to expand dramatic interviews, to concentrate on psychological detail and to write long, passionate speeches...".

[6] Of the 150 titles of tragedies listed for the period 1550—1620 by Elliott Forsyth in his *La Tragédie française de Jodelle à Corneille* (Paris, 1962), seventeen fall in the years 1550—1568, fifty-eight, between 1571 and 1599, and seventy-five, between 1600 and 1620.

We have already seen Hélisenne copy Boccaccio's descriptions of dawn to embellish her novel. Compared to the efforts of later humanists, these lines are rather insignificant. Montreux introduced the Fifth Day of his *Premier Livre des Bergeries de Juliette* with "Desia l'espouse de Titan auoit auancé la venuë du iour, fils du Soleil, & les herbes que elle auoit baignees de ses larmes humides, & argentees, cõmençoiët à se resiouir, & deuenir plus gayes qu'elles n'estoient auparauant, souz l'esperance de veoir la face ardante du soleil qui se leuoit encor de sa moitte couche, pour recommencer son cours ordinaire" (f. 212ᵛ). In tragedy, the humanists were even more verbose. Matthieu's description of the dawn in *Clytemnestre* occupies eighteen lines.

A further set piece at which so many humanists tried their hand was a description of the lady's beauty. The possible but not unique prototype may have been this passage from the *Arcadia*:

> Her tresses were covered with a veil most subtly thin, from under which two bright and beautiful eyes were flashing, not otherwise than the clear stars are wont to burn in the serene and cloudless sky. Her features, rather long in proportion than round, with lovely modelling, and of a whiteness not displeasing but moderate, almost shading into tan and accompanied with a graceful rosy flush, filled with desire the eyes that looked upon them. Her lips were such that they surpassed the morning rose; betwixt them, every time that she spoke or smiled, she showed some part of her teeth, of such an exotic and wondrous beauty that I would not have known how to liken them to anything other than orient pearls. From there descending to the delicate throat as smooth as marble, I saw on her tender bosom the small girlish breasts that like two round apples were thrusting forth the thin material . . . (p. 49)

Here is the description of Genievre which Belleforest chose to add to the text of the final tale in his first volume of the *Histoires Tragiques*:

> Vous eussiez veu ses tresses ondoyantes, & crespeluës, disposees de si bonne grace, qu'on eust iugé qu'Amour, & les trois Graces n'auoyent où ailleurs heberger, que par le contour de ceste belle, riche contournure, & enlacee liaison. En ces oreilles pendoyent deux belles & riches perles oriëtales, qui dõnoyent encor lustre à l'artifice des cheueux. Et qui eust contemplé le front serain & large de ceste Nymphe, sur lequel mignardement reluisoit vn beau & riche diamant, enchassé en vne tresse d'or, faite en forme de petites estoilles, il ne se fust persuadé autre cas, fors que de voir vn rang d'astres ardans, lorsque le ciel au plus chaud de l'Esté est serain, & descouurant l'ordre de ses

clous resplendissans. Aussi les yeux estincelans de la belle ornez de
ceste belle voute de deux arcs distinguez également, & teints d'vne
couleur d'Ebene, espandoyent si bien leur splendeur, que non plus
sont esbloüis ceux qui à plein midy contemplent directement le soleil,
qu'estoyent les yeux de ceux qui s'arrestoyent en la contemplation de
ces deux astres flamboyans, & qui ont la force de transpercer iusques
au plus profond des moüelles. Le nez bien pourfilé, & fait à l'égal
du surplus de la face, distinguoit les deux ioües teintes d'vn fin incar-
nat, ressemblant les petites pompes paruenues à leur entiere maturité:
& puis, sa bouche coraline, de laquelle respirant, sortoit vne haleine
plus soüefue & douce, que tout l'ambre & musc, ou autre drogue aro-
matique, que iamais l'Arabie ait engendré. Ceste-cy defermant quel-
quefois le serrail de ses léures, découuroit deux rangs de perles si
finement blanches, que l'Orient deuiendroit honteux, voulant paran-
gonner ce qu'il a de beau à ceste incomparable blancheur. Mais qui
adiousteroit la force du parler à tout cecy, il se pourroit vanter d'a-
uoir veu ce que nature fit onc de plus parfait. Or pour venir vn peu
plus bas, ceste Diane découuroit vne gorge qui faisoit honte à la
blancheur du lait, tant fust caillé: et son estomach vn peu releué par
les deux pommelus & fermes tetons, separez d'égale distance: estoit
couuert d'vn voile fort delié & subtil, & lequel presque n'empeschoit
point de voir ces petits gasons, haussans & rehaussans, selon l'affection qui se mouuoit au centre de la pensée de ceste modeste pucelle.
(I, 699—701)

In tragedy, comparable passages appear in Matthieu's *Clytemnestre*,
1589, p. 15, Behourt's *La Polyxène*, 1597, p. 23 [7], Le Jars' *Lucelle*,
1600, p. 12, Chrétien des Croix's *Amnon*, 1608, p. 53, Chevalier's
Philis, 1609, f. 12[r], and Billard's *Le Mérovée*, 1612, f. 55[v].

One demonstrable effect of the religious wars on the literature of
the period can be found in the number of tragedies dealing with
rebellion and with historical subjects taken from contemporary
history. Humanist prose shows us, however, that even with respect
to political subjects there is continuity here with the beginning of the
century. In the midst of Hélisenne's Part Two, she places this speech
in the mouth of a representative of a rebellious people, now subju-
gated by their prince with the help of Guenelic and Quezinstra:

Prince magnanime puis quil a pleu a vostre altitude dextirper de vr̃e
noble cueur la iuste yre que contre nous auiez conceue, & vous con-

---

[7] The passage in *La Polyxène* is all the more interesting since it is inspired by
Boaystuau's sixth translation from Bandello in the *Histoires Tragiques* but the
description in the play has no equivalent in the *Histoires Tragiques* text.

descendre a la facilite de pardonner, nonobstant la griefue offense par nous perpetree enuers vostre noblesse. Bien debuons estimer que vostre institution naturelle, & vraye gentillesse a ce faire vous prouocque: & aussy demonstrez que bien estez memoratif de ce que testifie & dit la saincte escripture, cest que ceulx sont felices qui seront misericords: car misericorde ilz ensuyront. Et par ce sentent qui nest chose plus apte a la fruytion de la vie bien heuree que est le oublier des facheries souffertes. Et a ceste occasion auons certaine euidence que ces euangelicques parolles sont en vostre cueur descriptes: que plus fermes en vng metail ne se pourroyent engrauer. Car considerant noz iniquitez, ne estoyt a presupposer pouuoir iamais trouuer paix ne reconciliation enuers vostre celsitude: mais vostre vrbanite a este superieure: & a este si puissante que elle a mitigue, & finablement adnichille la ferocite, ce qui vous doibt tourner en perpetuelle louenge: car entre les dons & graces de corps & de lame, celle seulle propre & peculiere vertu est ascripte a Cesar Auguste: duquel selon que puis concepuoir, vous estes vray exemplaire. Dont en ces considerations pouuons iuger tresfelice le peuple, sur lequel tel prince domine ... (II3r-v)

This interest should not surprise us. Many early humanistis like Erasmus and Rabelais were concerned about the education of princes and Adams has convincingly shown that such concern lay at the base of much criticism of medieval romances [8]. The humanists of the next generation shared that concern. Ronsard composed an *Institution pour l'adolescence du roy Charles IX*. In Montreux's *Amours de Cléandre et Domiphille*, a princess interjects in a story of love such thoughts as "l'Estat & le Prince sont tellement liez ensemble, que l'vn ne peut perir, sans traisner l'autre en son precipice ..." (f. 55r). In tragedy not only is rebellion a frequent subject but certain plays such as Matthieu's *Vasthi* (1589), Philone's *Adonias* (1586), and Faure's *Les Gordians et les Maximins* (1589) also devote extended discussion to the qualities of a good ruler.

Some of the preceding quotations are long and they were reproduced for a purpose. When critics speak about violence in late sixteenth-century French literature, they appear to refer to a dominant aspect of these works. In truth, we come much closer to sensing the tone of humanist writing when reading the long passages quoted above. They, and not the external events of war, murder, rebellion, or separation, fill the pages of humanist novels and plays. They do

---

[8] Robert P. Adams, "Bold Bawdry and Open Manslaughter: The English New Humanist Attack on Medieval Romance," *The Huntington Library Quarterly*, 23 (1959), 33—48.

so because on the one hand stylistic display was a most positive virtue but also because external events still derived their importance from the *commentary* or the *contemplation* that such events occasioned. There the author put into words the pedagogical import of his plot and arranged to exploit that plot in order to insert as many elements of concern as possible.

In the second half of the century a particularly interesting example of this technique is provided by Nicolas de Montreux's adaptation of the Greek novel.

Between 1595 and 1599 Montreux published the three books of his *Oeuvre de la chastete,* the story of the loves of Criniton and Lydie within which are related the adventures of a second couple, Cléandre and Domiphille. When prefacing his first volume Montreux included among his sources the Greek novels of Heliodorus and Achilles Tatius which were both rendered into French in the sixteenth century [9].

These two novels are characterized by the undying love of a young couple who until the final pages meet only with impediments to their wishes and attacks on their virtue. Tempests, pirates, and wars figure prominently among the means used to keep in motion a plot which seeks to entertain by suspending the revelation of key information and by creating ever new contexts for the action. The main couples have virtually no traits beyond their love and physical beauty. Development comes through outside factors. The threat to the couples' chastity, for example, is never the result of an inner failing but of an assault by people encountered in the course of their adventures. Despite the emphasis that is placed on chastity by the novels and the characters themselves, the text leaves no doubt that their love is rooted in passion [10]. In fact, to circumvent this desire, Chariclea makes Theagenes swear never to violate her honor before they are wed. In Achilles Tatius, Diana appears to both boy and girl in a

---

[9] See above, p. 10.

[10] I refer to such passages as this from Heliodorus: "Cependāt Chariclea & Theagenes demourerēt tous seulz dedans la cauerne ... ilz se saolerent d'acollades, d'embrassementz, & de baisers pris & donnez en priuauté tresfranche: & oubliantz à vn coup toutes leurs mesauentures, demeurerent vn long temps iointz l'vn à l'autre, ... prenantz à cueur saoul fruition de leur amour, chaste toutefois encore, & vierge, meslantz l'vn auecques l'autre leurs chaudes larmes seulement, & ne se ioignantz point de plus pres que des baisers netz & impolluz; Car quand Chariclea sentoit que Theagenes s'eschauffoit vn petit, & se vouloit monstrer homme, elle le refrenoit, en luy ramenant en memoire le serment qu'il auoit iuré, & luy se reprimoit, & se contenoit facilement, estant bien vaincu d'Amour: mais vainqueur de concupiscence" (ff. 51v—52r).

dream and warns them not to consummate their love until she has joined them in marriage.

In addition to the theme of chastity and the philosophizing which both translators of the Greek emphasized [9], a Frenchman like Montreux must have contemplated adapting the genre in view of even more fundamental links with the humanist tradition. Wolff has spoken of Heliodorus' conception of his novel as "a series of theatrical spectacles arranged by·superhuman agency" (p. 183). The characters are themselves so aware of the mighty hand of Fortune directing their fate that on occasion the novel gives rise to the kind of observation about Fortune and instability which is forthcoming in the didactic literature that inspired Hélisenne and in every genre attempted by the French humanists [11]. Descriptions of the pangs of love felt by Theagenes and Chariclea fill several pages and accentuate the same characteristics already familiar to the period [12]. Finally, the product of a very mannered moment in Greek letters, these novels enjoyed greatly creating and expressing paradox [13]. By the final decades of the sixteenth century, serious love verse had moved so far in the direction of a similar style, that I cannot believe Montreux was not impressed by such turns of phrase. At least it is fact that all such traits of the Greek novel inspired Montreux's own fiction.

There are also interesting ways in which the *Oeuvre de la chasteté* departs from its Greek models. In the same introduction to his first volume Montreux gives this revealing commentary on the difficulties

---

[11] For example, "O miserable fortune de la vie humaine, pleine de toute incõstance, & suiette à toute mutation! quel flux & reflux de miseres" (Heliodorus, f. 66ᵛ).

[12] Soon after seeing Chariclea for the first time, Theagenes is obliged to attend a banquet. But his thoughts are elsewhere: "tantost il regardoit contremont en l'ær, tantost il ietoit vn souspir du plus profond du cueur, sans aucune raison qui apparust, tantost il ietoit les yeux contre terre sans mot dire, comme vn homme qui pense fort profondemẽt quelque chose en soymesme, tantost il composoit tout soudain en vne autre contenance ioyeuse, & deliberée . . ." (f. 36ᵛ).

[13] Early in Achilles Tatius' novel a young man about to be married is thrown from his horse and dies. In a lament his father transforms the wedding symbols into the objects now attending his son; the nuptial couch has become a bier, the wedding torches are funeral brands. In Heliodorus, the concluding moments are heightened by such paradox as: "Elle appelloit son frere celuy qui ne l'estoit pas. Quand ie luy ay demãdé qui estoit ce ieune prisonnier, elle m'a dict qu'elle ne sçauoit: Et puis apres s'est efforcée de preseruer de la mort, comme son amy, celuy qu'elle ne congnoissoit point. Quãd elle a cogneu que sa demãde estoit impossible, elle m'a supplié luy permettre de l'occire, cõme s'il fust son mortel ennemy" (f. 117ʳ).

to be faced by his protagonists: "il n'est point de vertu plus louable, que celle qui parmy ses aduersaires paroist tousiours vertu, qui cŏbatue resiste, & ne perd son nom dans les abismes du vice, dont elle est attaquee. D'autant que la vertu sans aduersaires n'est digne de ce nom . . ." (*3ᵛ). This is *not* the perspective of the Greek novels. What they gain by giving the chaste pair sensual adversaries, they systematically destroy by refusing to create in the characters the moral strength to which Montreux alludes. The oath in Heliodorus, the dream in Achilles Tatius are only partial pieces of evidence in this regard. Of the four protgonists, one, Clitophon, in fact loses his chastity in the course of the novel — whence in Achilles Tatius, the ordeal for Leucippe alone as compared to ordeals in Heliodorus for both Chariclea and Theagenes to prove their purity. Clitophon has married Melite believing that his beloved is dead. He soon learns the truth but by then his wife is so distraught because their marriage is unconsummated that he sleeps with her: "aussi ce qui se passoit entre Melite [et moi] n'estoient point nopces, ains vne medecine que ie luy dŏnoy pour alleger son ame cŏme si elle eut esté languissante, & malade" (f. 98ʳ). A somewhat similar game is played in Heliodorus when Arsace steals a kiss from Theagenes: "Ainsi se partit Theagenes baisé d'elle, & nŏ pas elle baisée de luy" (f. 85ᵛ). Wolff provides a much more detailed discussion of the Greek protagonists but the preceding should suffice to indicate the disparity in tone between the Greek novels and Montreux.

The declaration that "la vertu sans aduersaires n'est digne de ce nom" has been heard before in this study; it is in effect the *sentence* out of which one of Quezinstra's key arguments evolves [14]. Montreux's interpretation of the basic plot of the Greek novels as a war between vice and virtue is even less surprising when we review further remarks made by Amyot as he introduces his translation of Heliodorus. The human passions are described, he says "auecques si grande honesteté, que lon n'en sçauroit tirer occasion, ou exemple de mal faire. Pource que de toutes affections illicites, & mauuaises, il a fait l'yssue malheureuse: & au contraire des bonnes, & honnestes, la fin desirable, & heureuse" (π2ᵛ—3ʳ). Even before entering the text, Montreux would have been predisposed to read moral commentary into the novel's dénouement. I prefer to believe, however, that the weight of evidence already presented is such as to make Montreux's reaction to the content of the Greek novels a logical conclusion within

---

[14] See above, p. 15.

humanist circles. It was perhaps abetted by but hardly dependent upon Amyot's introduction, itself a reflection of the same mentality.

Montreux's recasting of our perspective on the chastity theme is but the beginning of a more radical recasting of all the plot material. In summary form Montreux's novels appear as varied in their events as the Greek models. Tempests, wars, and pirates make their appearance here, too; but their role has changed. When Wolff speaks of a "series of theatrical spectacles", he is reminding us of the emphasis Heliodorus puts on many of his grand scenes. Heliodorus describes them in detail and the ever-changing contexts can be explained in part by the author's eagerness to prepare a new spectacle. Also, both Heliodorus and Achilles Tatius reflect in their works an ancestor of the Greek novel, the travel narration, in which flora, fauna, and mores of sites visited were duly described [15]. Montreux retains the means for animating the plot but suppresses the descriptive material and redefines the relationship between external events and the world of emotion. The events are introduced primarily, if not solely, to create a new emotional problem that Montreux can examine at length. The overall proportions between pages devoted to narrating events and to describing emotions show that Montreux greatly favored the latter.

I will give one example. In the first volume of his *Oeuvre de la chasteté*, Montreux devotes more than a hundred pages (pp. 287—400) to the analysis of emotions in Cléandre and Domiphille. The moment is prepared by Cléandre's capture and imprisonment in the house of Domiphille. It is used by Montreux to provoke in Cléandre a conflict between the force of love, quickened by Domiphille's proximity, and fear of displeasing her by speaking openly of his passion. For Domiphille the conflict is between love and honor. To love Cléandre constitutes a form of treason. Cléandre is an enemy of her people. It also makes her a rebellious child, for her father would never approve the match. Finally, she fears that this handsome stranger will betray her as Theseus and Jason did their respective loves. Hanging over these internal deliberations is the threat that Domiphille's people may condemn Cléandre to death. Domiphille resolves that her honor prevents her from helping an enemy escape but if her beloved is to die, she will kill herself. There can be no living without him.

---

[15] I refer to Achilles Tatius' analysis of the origin of a Bacchic rite (Book II) and of the habits of the crocodile (Book IV). Heliodorus' opening pages describe the mores of the brigands who capture Theagenes and Chariclea.

A second stage in these conflicts is reached when Cléandre realizes
to what degree Domiphille's position prevents her from giving him
any sign of affection. He decides to ease her pain by avoiding her
presence. Of course, the contrary result is produced as Domiphille
now fears that Cléandre no longer loves her. The death sentence is
pronounced — the only external event in these pages — and again a
happening serves to set in motion intense introspection. Certain he
will die, Cléandre feels that he can now reveal his love. Domiphille
will not betray her honor, however, and repulses the suitor. Cléandre
faints, is given up for dead. Domiphille suddenly faces a new crisis.
If she does not help Cléandre, she will have killed the man she loves;
if she runs to him, her gesture alone will reveal the emotions she had
just scorned. Domiphille decides to help the ailing lover but vows to
preserve her chastity — something Cléandre respects.

Although such proportions might suggest that Montreux had
broken somewhat with the moralizing of his contemporaries in favor
of the brand of character analysis for which French Classicism is
justly famous, the text does not permit such a sweeping conclusion. In
these analyses we are never far from the familiar truths about human
behavior whose expression is fundamental to the humanists' intent.
Here is Montreux's description of Oleande's reaction to the news
that her fiancé, once presumed dead, is in fact alive:

> Oleande à ceste nouuelle s'appaisa quelque peu, r'appellant l'esperan-
> ce qui s'en estoit fuye, & voulant viure encor pour dõner vie à son
> contentement esperé. Car les amants esperent tant qu'ils peuuent,
> mesme forgent eux mesmes des moyens d'esperãce, encor qu'ils soyent
> vains, d'autãt que sans ce bien il leur seroit impossible de viure, &
> que sur luy tout leur salut se repose, entre tant de peines, douleurs,
> & miseres que leur apporte le cruel amour, qui leur seroyent insup-
> portables & mortelles sans ce roc d'esperance, qui soustiẽt languissan-
> te leur vie, encor que souuẽt ce ne soit qu'vn ombre qui passe comme
> fumee, & qui n'a point de corps ny de vie seure. Oleãde donc reprist
> courage à ceste nouuelle, resolue d'employer tout ce qu'elle auroit de
> pouuoir pour me tirer de prison, & me rendre sien. Car on croit tous-
> iours qu'apres quelque perte ou disgrace adenuë par quelque faute,
> qu'on sera parapres sage & prudent à fuir la mesme erreur: dont en
> se corrigeant on se donne garde de faillir, plus pour euiter au mal
> où l'on s'est trouué miserablement englouty, autremẽt seroit viure en
> beste, & ne se destourner de la pierre où l'on heurte tousiours, tant
> qu'on se fust rompu le pied. (pp. 282—83)

The movement is simple. Montreux establishes that she reacted
with hope, reminds us at length that "les amants esperent tant qu'ils

peuuent", repeats the nature of Oleande's reaction (as if recognizing the quantity of commentary that goes before), and closes with an even more general observation by changing "les amants" to "on". Oleande's private hope lies buried beneath the hope of lovers and that of all men.

The preceding outline of certain humanist techniques serves us in two ways. It gives us an understanding of the artists' intent without which we cannot aspire to judge their works intelligently; it also provides a basis for appreciating to what degree the sixteenth century, intellectually as well as chronologically, lies between the Middle Ages and French Classicism.

In addition to Bouchet's *Les Angoysses et remedes d'amours*, another work on love popular at the time of Hélisenne de Crenne was Martial d'Auvergne's *Aresta amorum*. Both are not without elements that relate to Hélisenne or to Marguerite or later works of sixteenth-century fiction. For example, with Bouchet's traditional definition of love's effects and warning against idleness [16], should be mentioned a long praise of chastity (p. lxxvi). Beginning with a 1533 edition of the *Aresta*, Benoît de Court added detailed glosses of both a literary and legal nature. In the former we find Benoît accumulating Latin and Greek quotations to illustrate the familiar facts of love: "Amoris furor" (p. 10), "Amātes dura patiunter" (p. 30), "Amantes non dormiunt" (p. 147).

However, Bouchet and Martial chose to express themselves through the allegorical technique popularized by the *Roman de la Rose*. Martial's cases are tried in Love's Court; punished individuals are sometimes banished from Love's Kingdom. The poems which open Bouchet's work tell of adventures between a lover and such personifications as Jalousie, Faulx Semblant, Bon Espoir, and Refuz. The final section of the Bouchet work is composed of a long poem spoken by Pallas "aultrement appellee Raison" (p. liii). The humanists proceed otherwise. There are only people in Hélisenne's novel. The individuals may be one-dimensional and stereotyped; yet they are no longer the personifications of the *Roman de la Rose*.

The temptation to read metaphysical meanings into this demise of the allegory must be resisted. If the humanists preferred characters to allegorical figures, their characters were but human equivalents of many such allegorical types and the situations created by the earlier allegorists returned under the pen of the humanists, perhaps for the

---

[16] See above, p. 16.

simple reason that all were intent upon conveying the same truths. When Hélisenne tells the reader that reason came to aid her as she tried to resist love and said "comēt, veulx tu prēdre le villain chemin, ord & fetide, & laisser la belle sente, remplye de fleurs odoriferētes" (A5ʳ), we cannot call the novel an allegory but we cannot overlook either the obvious similarity in procedure and intent between this passage and Reason's role in the final section of Bouchet's work.

At the same time, the particular moral concerns of the humanists led them to develop other techniques diametrically opposed to those employed by French Classicists. In fiction as well as drama, action meant less to the humanists than the commentary occasioned by the action. Frank Hook, one of Belleforest's modern editors, provides a particularly telling insight into the humanist aesthetic when he observes that "Bandello, like his predecessor, Boccaccio, had a good sense of narrative technique; his stories move rapidly, often to atone for a poverty of plot. Belleforest seems to have had a positive genius for destroying the narrative movement of a story" (p. 11). Belleforest and his fellow humanists would not probably have used the term "destroy" to characterize their method of handling plot. The poems, the letters, the speeches that Belleforest added provided stylistic embellishment but also the expected and admired moralizing.

That humanist novels are quite long and humanist tragedies written in five acts does not constitute a situation in which tragedy comes closer to the Classical ideal. Both genres exibit the same interest in plot as an amalgam of events presented seriatim so that each can be examined for its pedagogical content. Not only is it rather useless to seek in humanist works the careful plot development that emerges from French Classical drama or *La Princesse de Clèves,* it is also unreasonable. The humanist was seeking to create effects which neither required nor encouraged a unity of action. When Amyot praised Heliodorus' novel because in it wicked acts breed unhappiness and upright deeds receive their desired end, he provided us with an excellent summary of the effect the humanists designed for the work as a whole [17]. Dénouement meant only outcome or result. It had

---

[17] Compare these statements by other French humanists of the day. Benigne Poissenot justifies the morality of his *Nouvelles Histoires tragiques* (Paris, 1586) by noting that "Les vices y sōt blasmez, on y loüe la vertue" (p. 11). Heudon introducing his *Pyrrhe* (Rouen, 1598) wrote of tragedies: "Sur vn trosne esleué s'y siera la vertu, / Si le vice s'y treuue, il sera combatu" (p. 11). In a preface to *Hypsicratée* (Rouen, 1604), Behourt speaks of "belles descriptions Heroïques, Tragiques, Comiques où sont representees comme en vn miroir l'excellence & recompense de la vertu, la laideur & punition du vice" (p. 6).

none of the overtones of unraveling, nor did it presuppose, as it did for the Classicists, the creation and *continued* manipulation of precise emotions in the reader or audience. The humanist procedure was discontinuous. Individual scenes are accorded great emphasis because the intention is to comment upon the matter at hand, not to propel the plot toward resolution or revelation. At best, we can speak of a unity of preoccupation or structure by dialectic, as in Hélisenne's novel, but we cannot find the subtle concatenation of events and emotions that characterizes French Classicism.

MONTREUX AND THE PASTORAL

The preceding has done more than assure us that the sixteenth century possessed a particularly wide-spread concept of literary expression which distinguishes it from both the medieval and Classical periods in French letters. That concept also provides a means to explain why the prose analyzed by Reynier yielded so little of what he sought.

Reynier presents the situation as a mystery. The writers knew and admired ancient texts which might have inspired them to produce "romans sentimentaux" but they remained strangely unresponsive, "incapable" of developing such material, to paraphrase Reynier. Yet, there is a mystery here only as long as we do not sense to what degree the French writers in question were reading their potential sources within an aesthetic context that channeled their impressions and directed their thoughts away from the sentimental novel. Hélisenne's excesses in her style are no accident. Marguerite involves her *devisants* with their stories for a reason as fundamental to her purpose as was Montreux's decision to transform the vagaries of fortune into a test of virtue. Where we may speak of these writers as "incapable" is in recognizing their lack of desire to disavow literature that treats sentiment as the handmaiden of *sententiae* and plot as the mere enactment of moral truths.

The strength of such beliefs which were capable of determining the nature of sixteenth-century tragedy and short stories as well as novels has much to say about a final problem raised in the Introduction: the history of the pastoral tradition. Reynier believed that the development of the sentimental novel in general was interrupted by the religious wars to recommence only with the return of peace and the establishment of a new social milieu (p. 341). By pointing to early French translations of the *Arcadia* and of Montemayor's *Diana* which, nevertheless, achieved prominence only with the publication of *l'Astrée*, Reynier makes treatment of the pastoral novel a prime proof of his theory.

Given that Montreux began to publish his *Bergeries de Juliette* in 1585 and included in the first volume his pastoral play *Athlète*, I think it is somewhat excessive to say that the French translation of the *Diana* in 1578 "ne semble pas avoir alors d'influence" (Reynier, p. 167). An analysis of these works by Montreux shows also that the appearance of the *Diana* in 1578 brought it into contact with (perhaps into competition with) the humanist aesthetic we have been studying and I am inclined to believe that the initial fate of the pastoral tradition must be examined from the point of view of existing literary conventions rather than the disruption caused by the religious wars.

The "Arguments" that Montreux wrote to introduce his pastoral plays *Athlète* and *Diane* suggest very animated plots. Basic to both plays are the elements of magic and unrequited love which produce an initial crisis that will be resolved happily. In Montreux's first pastoral, a magician plots to murder her rival (Athlète) with a poisoned apple in the hope that Menalque will then turn to her. Instead, after the apple is eaten, she watches horrified as Menalque prepares to follow Athlète in death. Through more magical potions Athlète is resuscitated and the magician cured of her passion. In *Diane* a magician is engaged by one of the sheperds (Fauste) to assist him in winning a promise of marriage from the girl he loves. He succeeds but when Diane discovers the deception and upbraids Fauste, the shepherd attempts suicide. Diane is so moved that she returns to Fauste whom she had once loved and abandoned for another. Through a *scène de reconnaissance* and more magic, the remaining characters also find a happy end to their difficulties.

The action seems animated, but as with Montreux's novels, such summaries can be misleading. The plays are filled with long speeches, some devoted to the sentimental problems posed, all written to exhibit Montreux's skill in rhetoric. *Athlète* opens with a description by the magician of her art and cave. No other character speaks. The second scene begins with a lament by Rustic and when Menalque arrives to comfort his lamenting friend, he sings of his own loves and describes

44

a terrible dream he has had. Descriptions, dreams, laments, they are the stuff of these pastoral dramas to which we must add the debate.

In a scene from Act I of *Diane*, for example, two shepherds discuss a question that is hardly unfamiliar to humanist literature: can man determine his own fate or is the god of love all-powerful. The rhetorical quality of the scene is made evident by the construction of the arguments. Each shepherd is first accorded four verses, then two, then one.

Some may object that the particular qualities of Montreux's adaptations derive simply from the dramatic conventions of the day and would pertain to all material, including the pastoral. Were it not for the existence of Tasso's *Aminta*, the objection would hold.

Athlète was published in the year following the appearance in Paris of the *Aminta*, first in Italian and then in a French translation. Such a rapid sequence of events may exclude the possibility that Montreux knew of Tasso's work when conceiving of *Athlète* and may explain why there is no resemblance between the works [1]. The same explanation cannot be applied in the case of *Diane*, however. *Diane* was composed nearly a decade after *Aminta* became available to the French; and yet, as we have just seen, Montreux's two pastoral plays do not differ substantially in conception. Only the attempted suicide in *Diane* and its happy consequences recall *Aminta*, whereas in virtually every other aspect Montreux's plays depart from the pastoral scene as it was portrayed by Tasso.

Aminta contains no magic and only four major characters of whom Sylvia and Aminta alone are troubled by love. *Athlète's* plot turns on the sentimental problems of no fewer than four characters. In *Diane* the number rises to five (not including the magician). This distinction in the number of *dramatis personae* corresponds to an even greater distinction in the concept of plot. If Tasso's play contains the fewest characters, it is because he knows how to derive the entire drama from their situation. On the one hand, Aminta and Sylvia are confronted by the worldly advice of the older couple; on the other, they are experiencing within themselves the turmoil of a budding love. Only a satyr was added to make the plot complete.

In good humanist fashion, Montreux shows himself to be interested neither in a simple plot nor in simple language. Whereas by making the length of the play correspond to the critical period in his charac-

---

[1] The dedication in Pierre de Brach's translation is dated 27 August 1584; the privilege for Montreux's *Athlète*, 14 June 1585.

ters' development, Tasso was providing a technical innovation that Mairet and French Classicism would come to appreciate, Montreux continues to treat plot as a source of elegant speeches and debates, constantly moving out from the story, constantly dissolving the action into lyricism and commentary. The contrast in technique is particularly strong in Tasso's refusal to use magic and in Montreux's reliance upon it. There is no magic in *Aminta* because the evolution of events proves indistinguishable from the evolution of emotions. Born of the inner conflicts of Sylvia and Aminta, the plot is resolved when the characters resolve these conflicts. Although magic appears in sources of the pastoral tradition, Montreux may have used it for another reason. He begins his plays with complexities that could have been handled in the manner chosen by Tasso but instead develops them in the direction of poetic and didactic display, that is, with the humanists' preference for broad truths over any particular revelations about each individual which could justify whatever change of heart would later prove necessary if the plot were to reach some happy outcome. Since such changes of heart must occur in *Athlète* and *Diane*, magic provides the cure for character *and* author.

It is not enough, I believe, to recognize in Montreux's pastoral plays certain traits of the humanist aesthetic; we must add that Montreux opted for such a technique over the alternative model furnished by Tasso [2]. The choice suggests what history confirms. France was not yet receptive to the simplicity or the subtlety of *Aminta*. They would have to await the seventeenth century for their flowering. Meanwhile, the traits peculiar to the pastoral world proved easy to adapt to existing modes. The magicians boasted of their art with the same flourish as the tyrants of humanist tragedy. A love plot stimulated familiar complaints and familiar discussions. I see no simple or logical means to bring the religious wars into play here. In fact, when Montreux presented *Le Premier Livre des Bergeries de Juliette*, his justification for the work shows to what degree the wars *stimulated* interest in literature: "Si tu t'estonne, amy Lecteur", writes Montreux, "de quoy en vn tẽps plein de guerres & de calamitez ciuilles, i'ay voulu mettre ce liure en lumiere, veu que les lettres restent muettes & sans vigueur parmy la force & les armes, ie t'ameneray seulement en ieu, pour toute response, l'histoire d'Alexandre, qui ... au plus fort de ses combats, auoit tousiours derriere le

---

[2] It is of some interest to recognize that Guarini's *Pastor Fido* exhibits the same general traits as Montreux's adaptations and that students of the pastoral have long considered Guarini's play *the* model for French and English pastoral dramas.

cheuet de son lict, auec son espée, l'Illiade d'Homere... Aussi que les lettres & les loix, ne sont tant necessaires en aucune saison, qu'en celle de la guerre..." (ã5ʳ⁻ᵛ).

In *Les Bergeries de Juliette,* a prose work, Montreux imitates in structure and content the *Diana* of Montemayor. Here, as Urfé would do in *l'Astrée,* the author devotes an initial period of each chapter to the complex love stories of the shepherds and then moves to a story told by one of them before the assembled group. The plot which treats of the shepherds contains no surprises. The usual chain formed of lovers who each pine for an individual who pines for another or for no one is exploited, broken, and reformed by perfectly conventional means. With the short stories, the resemblance to Montemayor ceases.

In the *Diana* (and *l'Astrée*) the interpolated stories recount adventures that have befallen the same characters who belong to the pastoral plots. In *Les Bergeries de Juliette* the stories possess no such ties to the main plot. They are set in France, Italy, and Spain and belong to the tradition of sixteenth-century *novelle.* Why Montreux made this change can be only a matter for conjecture; the popularity of Bandello's short stories could provide an answer in itself. What remains a fact is that Montreux imitated but a part of the *Diana* and filled out his *Bergeries* with a popular, yet foreign element [3].

Since Marguerite and Belleforest have shown to what degree that foreign element could be adapted to the humanist aesthetic, a second conjecture — already suggested by Montreux's pastoral plays — is that the love stories which open each day of the *Bergeries* and the *nouvelles* that close them belonged together in the eyes of the period because they were felt to portray similar phenomena. There is no little evidence in the text of the *Premier Livre des Bergeries de Juliette* to support that second conjecture.

Montreux announced on his title page that "par les amours des Bergers & Bergeres, l'on void les effects differents de l'amour". Later, when it comes time to move from the lives of the shepherds to the short story of the day, the transition on each of the first three days involves a long preamble on the same effects of love. The number of didactic phrases employed to introduce the story may vary but where the storyteller enters into commentary, we read the time-worn truths. On the first day, these verses are quoted from a poem composed by

---

[3] Even Montreux's title underlines the separation: *Le Premier Livre des Bergeries de Ivlliette... auec cinq histoires Comiques, racontées en cinq Iournées, par cinq Bergeres...*

one of the characters in the story to come: "Et la loy que le ciel, aux amoureux impose / C'est que iamais leur cœur sous l'espoir ne repose." They occasion immediately this observation, "Voila la doctrine que l'amour enseigne à l'ouuerture de son escolle aux premiers disciples, & voila le fascheux commencement de sa discipline, que le temps consommeur de toutes choses, rĕd à la fin si aisé, qu'il ne s'est gueres trouué d'amants, qui se soiĕt repĕtiz d'auoir aimé . . ." (f. 25ᵛ). On the third day, the storyteller begins by saying that to some the account may seem unbelievable, "Mais d'autant qu'elle est autrefois aduenuë, & que ce fut par la puissance d'amour, auquel le pouuoir humain ne peut s'oposer, . . . i'ay pĕsé que chacun de vous l'estimera vraye comme elle est, & en outre qu'elle est digne d'estre ouye, pour estre toute plaine des accidens diuers, qui procedent de l'amour, qui est vne cupidité irraisonnable . . ." (f. 124ʳ⁻ᵛ).

Interestingly enough, Montreux's prose can on occasion approach the analysis of human emotion in which Classicism was to excel. Here is his description of Lydie in a moment of crisis:

> Ce qui la tourmente dauantage, c'est qu'vn *[sic]* autre s'en esiouït, qui n'a si iustement merité qu'elle, le bien qu'elle pert, & ce qui la tuë, c'est de se voir vne autre preferee, qu'elle estime moindre qu'elle, son sang boult d'ardeur, son sein tressaut de furie, son ame vague dans ses esprits vitaux, incĕsee, & cõme rauie de fureur, sõ cœur fremit de furieux despit, & sa face pallist de fiere vĕgeance, elle iniurie son ame, de croire vray ce qui l'afflige en son estre, & le veut croire pour satisfaire à sa rage. Elle se fasche de perdre ce qu'elle estimoit plus cher que sa vie, & la veut perdre pour nourrir son despit & sa haine. Elle se fasche de se fascher pour la perte d'vne chose, qu'elle estime indigne de sa cholere, & pendant veut se douloir de sa perte, pour satisfaire au regret qui la tuë. Toutes choses luy semblent ennemyes, puis que c'elle *[sic]* est d'elle estimee mortelle aduersaire, dont elle pensoit estre seule aymee sans mesure d'affection. Elle tasche de l'aymer encore, pour plaire à son desir, & veut en tirer vengeance, pour satisfaire à l'amour outragé.

> (*Oeuvre de la chasteté*, p. 57)

Did he learn such analysis from the pastoral? It is possible. But we cannot let these passages efface the considerable devaluation of the pastoral material that occurs in *Athlète* or *Les Bergeries de Juliette*. In neither case does Montreux permit his use of new subject matter to effect a break with the style and intent of the humanist aesthetic. That later French writers of similar pastoral plays such as Montchrétien and Chrétien des Croix also produced tragedies in the vein of Garnier or Montreux shows how natural this adaptation appeared long after 1585. Tasso, not Montreux, proves the exception among sixteenth-century reactions to *Arcadia* and the *Diana*. There is involved here an element of literary genius, to be sure. But admitting that Montreux possessed the less powerful, less innovative imagination merely proves an alternative means to accentuate the hold of a predefined approach to literature upon France in these years.

Moreover, just as there seems little reason to attribute to the religious wars what may be explained by the vitality of the humanist aesthetic, so we should not confuse the rise of the pastoral in prose and drama following the end of the wars with the beginnings of Classicism [4]. Pastoral plays and the tragi-comedy (two very similar phenomena) will tend to disappear together as the Classical theatre comes into being [5]. It may be necessary in the future to see the study of love as a continuum in French letters punctuated by the humanist and Classical aesthetic among others. Each momentarily surrounds the subject with considerations of style, purpose, *vraisemblance* which reshape its presentation without inhibiting the development that comes from the constant handling of such material. Whatever is the definitive source of Montreux's inspiration, these essays would suggest that the coming of French Classicism may be more closely related to the fate of the humanist aesthetic in seventeenth-century France than to the success of the pastoral.

CONCLUSION

Since it has not been possible to discuss certain specific problems surrounding *Les Angoysses douloureuses* or the pastoral tradition in France without alluding to a humanist aesthetic which is distinct from medieval allegory and from French Classicism, I would hope that these essays have demonstrated conclusively the great danger inherent in studying sixteenth-century literature in the light of seventeenth-century accomplishments. We run the risk of concluding that the

---

[4] See, for example, the chapter entitled "La Pastorale et les origines du théâtre classique" in Jules Marsan, *La Pastorale dramatique en France* (Paris, 1905), pp. 335—392.

[5] See Henri-Jean Martin, *Livre: Pouvoirs et Société à Paris au XVIIe Siècle (1598—1701)*, 2 vols. (Geneva, 1969) II, 1077, and H. C. Lancaster, *A History of French Dramatic Literature*, (Baltimore, 1929), Part I, vol. 2, 449.

earlier writers were incapable of achieving what the 1600's produced and of failing to understand how unfair such a comparison is since it postulates some identity in intention where none can be found. Unfair, the comparison is equally harmful. Because it presupposes an identity in intention, it does not stimulate a search for answers to those problems that arise when the sixteenth century departs from expected behavior.

Of the various answers proposed above, thanks to recent work by Griffin on Du Bellay, by Jondorf and Griffiths on tragedy [1], we are perhaps no longer surprised by the prominence of rhetoric in determining sixteenth-century style and structure. The similarity in preoccupation between fiction and emblem literature is a domain much less studied to date. Yet I believe that it can explain as much in these works as rhetoric has done.

French emblem books printed during the sixteenth century vary in their format. In a translation of Alciati a motto is placed above the picture and a short poem beneath. Corrozet adds a longer poem on the facing page. La Perrière has no motto or poem with the picture but retains the verses on the facing page. Thus in all these cases we have a picture accompanied by some explanatory poetry. The picture is usually quite rudimentary; the poetry, without distinction. Still, any tendency for the modern eye to dismiss these works as too simple to have been important for the period's major artists must be strenuously resisted. The use by Maurice Scève of such pictures in his *Délie*, a work of several dense and complex poems, provides an initial warning.

More impressive is the general agreement of art historians when studying the École de Fontainebleau or other contemporary French painters and sculptors that all were capable of reproducing emblematic elements in their most elaborate works of art — an approach based no doubt on the occasional directness of the artists themselves [2]. One engraving by Jean Mignon depicts Abraham's sacrifice of Isaac. The work exhibits the florid quality of the École de Fontainebleau;

---

[1] Robert Griffin, *Coronation of the Poet: Joachim Du Bellay's Debt to the Trivium,* (Berkeley and Los Angeles, 1969); Gillian Jondorf, *Robert Garnier and the Themes of Political Tragedy in the Sixteenth Century,* (Cambridge, Eng., 1969); Richard Griffiths, *The Dramatic Technique of Antoine de Montchrestien,* (Oxford, 1970).

[2] I think of such studies as Naomi Miller, "The Form and Meaning of the Fontaine des Innocents," *The Art Bulletin* 50 (1968), 270—77; and Jacques Thuillier, "L'Enigme de Félix Chrestien," *Art de France* I (1961), 57—74.

yet in the foreground of the sacrifice scene Mignon discreetly placed the short Latin phrase "PLACVIT DEVM OBEDIENTIA" [3]. We may be far from the emblem books in the quality of the artistic expression but when we view the scene through its moral, we return immediately to the world of Alciati and Corrozet.

Fundamental to the emblem book is the notion that the picture represented should be "read". Its parts could each have significance but the total work had its message also — summarized by the motto that usually accompanied the picture. La Perrière's eighteenth emblem shows a naked woman holding a key in her right hand; a finger of her left hand is placed against her lips and her right foot rests on a turtle. The poem accompanying the emblem reminds the reader that:

> Par la tortue, entendre est de besoing,
> Que la femme honneste aller ne doit pas loing,
> Le doigt leue, qu'a parler ne s'auance,
> La clef en main, denote qu'auoir soing
> Doit sur les biens du mary, par prudence.

Belleforest was thoroughly familiar with this definition of the prudent woman and demonstrates the period's sensitivity to the emblem books by incorporating into his translation of a Bandello tale this passage (designed to describe the female protagonist): "Cette dame sembloit auoir estudié en la theologie des Egyptiens: qui nous peignoyent vne Venus, tenant vne clef deuant sa bouche, & le pied sur la tortue: nous signifians par cela le deuoir de la femme pudique: la langue de laquelle doit estre noüee, ne parlant qu'en temps & lieu, & les pieds non vagabonds" (I, 516—17) [4].

Panofsky's work on iconology has shown that such paintings of the period as Jean Cousin's "Eva prima Pandora" also possess ample material for "reading". The serpent wound about one of Eve's arms and the branch in her hand help identify the first woman. Two vases, one held shut by Eve, the other spouting smoke in the background, add the necessary Pandora dimension. They are the vases of good and evil. The cloud that issues from the open vase represents the evil which Eve/Pandora let into the world. Finally, Eve rests on a skull.

---

[3] The work is reproduced in Henri Zerner's *The School of Fontainebleau: Etchings and Engravings*, (New York, 1969), J. M. 54.

[4] The reference to the Egyptians provides another link to the emblems. A reading of Horapollo convinced writers of emblem books that Egyptian hieroglyphics were, in truth, emblems.

Panofsky shows the relationship in the contemporary mind between Pandora and the Fall of Man by quoting Henri Estienne, who equated Prometheus and Adam, Eve and Pandora and the theft of fire with the eating of the fruit that gave man knowledge of good and evil. I would be more inclined to find the meaning of the skull in the words from Genesis, "In the day that thou eatest [of the tree of knowledge] thou shalt surely die" (2:17). Be that as it may, there is no avoiding a deliberate effort by Cousin to accumulate individual symbols in order to reinforce the truth that the story of Eve is analogous to that of Pandora.

Two paintings from the École de Fontainebleau furnish an intriguing glimpse of how this technique relates to the fiction we have been studying. The works are variations on a single scene in which a beautiful woman handles her jewels and is reflected in a mirror that stands to her left [5]. The artist or artists is unknown; the title, a matter of speculation. The woman has sometimes been called Diane de Poitiers, as happens frequently but without justification to lovely, unidentified ladies painted during this period. A number of facts point rather to the possibility of interpreting the paintings as an allegory of vanity and lust. De Tervarent lists vanity as a definite attribute of both jewelry and mirrors in painting between 1450 and 1600. The mirror was also associated with lust. A woodcut by Hans Brosamer (c. 1500—c. 1554) entitled "Die Eitelheit und Narrheit" depicts a naked woman with jewels about her neck, a mirror in one hand and an elegant container (the goblet of Dürer's "Nemesis"?) in the other. A man dressed as a fool lies at her feet [6]. Finally, in both French works, the mirror is supported by a naked man and woman. The Copenhagen canvas shows the figures embracing.

If our ignorance concerning the origins of these paintings will not permit a positive assertion as to the artist's intent, two prose works we have already mentioned reveal that the scene depicted had long entered the world of fiction with the precise symbolism suggested by the iconology of the period. Early in the *Fiammetta*, Boccaccio undertakes to define the moral transformation that love brings to his

---

[5] One painting hangs in the Musée Municipal at Dijon. It has been reproduced in Pierre Quarré, *Le Musée de Dijon*, (Paris, 1948). The other is part of the L. Christiansen Collection in Copenhagen. It is reproduced in G. F. Hartlaub, *Zauber des Spiegels*, (Munich, 1951), fig. 68. The popularity of the Dijon pose in particular is attested to by a similar figure in the Worcester, Massachusetts Art Museum. See *Art through Fifty Centuries: From the Collections of the Worcester Art Museum*, (Worcester, 1948), fig. 74.

[6] Hartlaub, fig. 148.

heroine. Here are her words of confession: "Semblablement les parures & ornemens, desquels du commencement ie ne me souciois pas cõme ayant peu affaire d'iceux, me commencerent à agreer, pensant qu'estant braue, ie plairois dauantage: & pour cete cause, ie feis cas des vestemens, de l'or, des perles, & d'autres choses precieuses plus que iamais … & iamais ie ne sortois de ma chambre, sans premierement prendre l'asseuré conseil de mon miroir …" (f. 27^{r-v}). Hélisenne copies both intent and symbols. She declares: "incontinent que ie leuz veu, ie me retiray vng petit, affin de prẽdre conseil a mõ miroir, de mõ accoustrement, grace, & cõtenance." And then, to drive home the moral, the husband exclaims: "Ie vous vois vser de regardz dissolus & impudiques, & estes si perturbee, que raison ne domine plus en vous" (Bl^{v}).

It would not be easy to find in sixteenth-century art so remarkable an equivalent for all the scenes in contemporary fiction but we have learned enough in the preceding essays to recognize that the principle of teaching an abstract truth through the representation of some human situation was as common to literature as it was to art. Between "reading" the "Eva prima Pandora" and contemplating the lessons outlined by Marguerite's *devisants* or announced by Hélisenne herself, there is very little difference — an analogy that must deepen our appreciation of other aspects of the humanist aesthetic, namely the discontinuity in structure and the relationship between character and story.

The procedure of immediately coupling events with some general commentary appears even more natural in an environment where emblem books and painting also accustomed the readers to translate scenes into lessons. Similarly, however problematic the juxtaposition of a languid lover and a valiant soldier may appear today to those who read Hélisenne, we cannot deny that Guenelic's languid state and Quezinstra's victories surround the characters with the same kind of symbolic material Hélisenne used in Part One to define love's effect on her. There is considerable posturing in these novels. The most dramatic moments — the debate, the lament, the confession — are related to rhetorical display. But it may not be idle to reflect on the number of secondary scenes that reappear: indiscreet acts, sleepless nights, thoughts of suicide. They flesh out the plot with those facts that Benoît de Court felt worthy of a gloss [7] and which, by virtue of the remarkable similarity between these glosses and emblem mottoes,

---

[7] See above, p. 41.

illustrate how close this fiction comes to building its story on the individual truths the century continually associated with love.

Studies of the sixteenth century, especially work done in France, have often preferred to play down these phenomena in favor of the "Renaissance" signs: the nude in "Eva prima Pandora" versus the skull, the Italian decoration in architecture versus the medieval structures [8]. Yet the texts, the paintings themselves give the lie to the validity of any severe shift of emphasis toward "Renaissance" signs. Who is to say that we should forget the serpent, the branch, the skull, the vases, the title in "Eva prima Pandora" to contemplate only the reclining woman? How can we separate the overtly didactic emblem books from the supposedly entertaining *Histoires Tragiques* when Belleforest incorporates into Bandello's text the emblematic description of the prudent woman? To be sure, saying that the situations of many novels and tragedies are like emblems does not assure us that the intention of the writer was to compose emblems in prose and verse. It does, however, reinforce the idea that there was considerable aesthetic unity in the century by showing that such unity resided in a common mentality: portraying the human animal meant showing and stating the simple generalities that summarized human existence. Man's inner world belonged to, was determined by the familiar symbols that spoke such generalities. The tales about him were in the main not constructed, conceived, or written to convey any illusion of psychological reality but rather a one-to-one relationship between event (or emotion) and the apothegm it exemplified. In the humanist aesthetic, it is extremely difficult to distinguish between teaching and pleasing. When we sense, therefore, with what insistence the Classicists spoke of *plaire*, how richly they endowed the inner world of their characters, and how discreet, hidden even, is the "message" of their great works, we have recognized again that French humanism and French Classicism are very distinct aesthetics.

---

[8] Compare Panofsky's analysis of "Eva prima Pandora" with these remarks by Louis Gillet in *La Peinture française: Moyen Age et Renaissance*, (Paris, 1928): "Pour la première fois, la nudité apparaît comme motif avoué du tableau et comme condition expresse de la beauté. Quelques restes de symbolisme qu'on puisse signaler çà et là dans l'ouvrage, c'est le premier manifeste français de l'indépendance de l'art" (p. 51).

BIBLIOGRAPHY

Achilles Tatius, *Les Amours de Clitophon et de Leucippe*. Trans. François de Belleforest. Paris, 1575.

Alciati, Andrea, *Livret des emblemes*. Trans. J. Le Fèvre. Paris, 1536.

Belleforest, François de, trans., *Histoires tragiques extraites des œuvres italiennes de Bandel*. 7 vols. Rouen, 1603—04.

Boccaccio, Giovanni, *The Decameron*. Trans. Frances Winwar. New York, 1955.

—, *La Fiammette amoureuse*. Paris, 1585.

Bouchet, Jean, *Les Angoysses et remedes d'amours*. Poitiers, [1536].

Corrozet, Gilles, *Hecatomgraphie*. Paris, 1541.

Daele, Rose-Marie, *Nicolas de Montreulx*. New York, 1946.

Demats, Paule (see under Hélisenne de Crenne).

De Tervarent, Guy, *Attributs et Symboles dans l'art profane 1450—1600*. 2 vols. Geneva, 1958.

Du Bellay, Joachim, *La Deffence et illustration de la langue françoyse*. Ed. Henri Chamard. 3rd. ed. Paris, 1966.

Du Souhait, Sieur, *Tragédie de Radégonde*. Rouen, 1606.

Heliodorus, *L'Histoire aethiopique*. Trans. J. Amyot. Paris, 1559.

Hélisenne de Crenne, *Les Angoysses douloureuses qui procedent d'amours*. Paris, n. d. (From Demats' description of the various printings of the *Angoysses*, this appears to be a copy of the second edition, distinct from the original 1538 volume and from the 1541 printing by Pierre Sergent.) All quotations are from this edition.

—, *Les Angoysses douloureuses qui procedent d'amours*. Première Partie. Ed. Paule Demats. Paris, 1968.

Hook, Frank, ed., *The French Bandello*. Columbia, Missouri, 1948.

Jourda, Pierre, *Marguerite d'Angoulême*. 2 vols. Paris, 1930.

Krailsheimer, A. J., "The Heptameron Reconsidered", in *The French Renaissance and its Heritage: Essays presented to Alan M. Boase*. Ed. D. R. Haggis. London, 1968, pp. 75—92.

La Perrière, Guillaume de, *Le Theatre des bons engins*. Paris, 1539.

Le Maçon, Antoine, trans., *Le Decameron de Messire Iehan Boccace*. Paris, 1545.

Marguerite de Navarre, *L'Heptaméron*. Ed. Michel François. Paris, [1950].

[Martial d'Auvergne], *Aresta amorum*. Lyons, 1538. All quotations are from this edition.

—, *Les Arrêts d'amour*. Ed. Jean Rychner. Paris, 1951.

Matthieu, Pierre, *Clytemnestre*. Lyons, 1589.

Montreux, Nicolas de, *Les Amours de Cléandre et Domiphille*. Paris, 1598.
—, *Athlète*. Paris, 1587.
—, *La Diane*. Tours, 1594.
—, *Oeuvre de la chasteté* [Les Amours de Criniton et Lydie]. Paris, 1587.
—, *Le Premier Livre des Bergeries de Juliette*. Paris, 1587.

Panofsky, Dora and Erwin, *Pandora's Box*. New York, 1956.

Reynier, Gustave, *Le Roman sentimental avant l'Astrée*. Paris, 1908.

Sannazaro, Jacopo, *Arcadia and Piscatorial Eclogues*. Trans. Ralph Nash. Detroit, 1966.

Wolff, Samuel Lee, *The Greek Romances in Elizabethan Prose Fiction*. New York, 1912.

Woodward, William H., *Desiderius Erasmus concerning the Aim and Method of Education*. Cambridge, Eng., 1904.

Attention is called to P. Brockmeier's *Lust und Herrschaft: Studien über gesellschaftliche Aspekte der Novellestik von Boccaccio, Sachetti, Marguerite von Navarra*, Stuttgart, 1972, which unfortunately appeared too late to be considered before these essays went to press.